PENGUIN BOOKS — GREAT IDEAS

On Friendship

Michel de Montaigne

1533–1592

Michel de Montaigne

On Friendship

TRANSLATED BY M. A. SCREECH

PENGUIN BOOKS — GREAT IDEAS

PENGUIN BOOKS

Published by the Penguin Group
Penguin Books Ltd, 80 Strand, London WC2R ORL, England
Penguin Group (USA) Inc., 375 Hudson Street, New York, New York 10014, USA
Penguin Books Australia Ltd, 250 Camberwell Road,
Camberwell, Victoria 3124, Australia
Penguin Books Canada Ltd, 10 Alcorn Avenue, Toronto, Ontario, Canada M4V 3B2
Penguin Books India (P) Ltd, 11 Community Centre,
Panchsheel Park, New Delhi – 110 017, India
Penguin Group (NZ), Cnr Airborne and Rosedale Roads,
Albany, Auckland 1310, New Zealand
Penguin Books (South Africa) (Pty) Ltd, 24 Sturdee Avenue,
Rosebank 2196, South Africa

Penguin Books Ltd, Registered Offices: 80 Strand, London WC2R ORL, England

www.penguin.com

This translation first published in Penguin Classics 1991
This edition published in Penguin Books 2004

5

Translation copyright © M.A. Screech. 1991
All rights reserved

The moral right of the translator has been asserted

Taken from the Penguin Classics edition of *The Complete Essays*,
translated and introduced by M. A. Screech

Set in Monotype Dante
Typeset by Rowland Phototypesetting Ltd, Bury St Edmunds, Suffolk
Printed in England by Clays Ltd, St Ives plc

Contents

I

On friendship

I was watching an artist on my staff working on a painting when I felt a desire to emulate him. The finest place in the middle of a wall he selects for a picture to be executed to the best of his ability; then he fills up the empty spaces all round it with *grotesques*, which are fantastical paintings whose attractiveness consists merely in variety and novelty. And in truth what are these *Essays* if not monstrosities and *grotesques* botched together from a variety of limbs having no defined shape, with an order sequence and proportion which are purely fortuitous?

Desinit in piscem mulier formosa superne.
[A fair woman terminating in the tail of a fish.]*

I can manage to reach the second stage of that painter but I fall short of the first and better one: my abilities cannot stretch so far as to venture to undertake a richly ornate picture, polished and fashioned according to the rules of art. So I decided to borrow a 'painting' from Etienne de La Boëtie, which will bring honour to the

* Horace, *Ars poetica* 4. (Poets can create monsters at will; say a fair maid with the tail of a fish, that is, a mermaid.)

I

rest of the job: I mean the treatise to which he gave the title *On Willing Slavery* but which others, not knowing this, very appropriately baptised afresh as *Against One*. He wrote it, while still very young, as a kind of essay against tyrants in honour of freedom. It has long circulated among men of discretion – not without great and well-merited esteem, for it is a noble work, as solid as may be. Yet it is far from being the best he was capable of. If, at the age when I knew him when he was more mature, he had conceived a design such as mine and written down his thoughts, we would now see many choice works bringing us close to the glory of the Ancients; for, particularly where natural endowments are concerned, I know nobody who can compare with him. Yet nothing of his survives apart from this treatise – and even that is due to accident: I do not think he ever saw it again once he let go of it – and some *Considerations* on that *Edict of January* which our civil wars have made notorious: I may perhaps still find a place for it elsewhere. That is all I have been able to recover of his literary remains, I the heir to whom, with death on his lips, he so lovingly willed his books and his papers – apart from the slim volume of his works which I have had published already.

Yet I am particularly indebted to that treatise, because it first brought us together: it was shown to me long before I met him and first made me acquainted with his name; thus preparing for that loving-friendship between us which as long as it pleased God we fostered so perfect and so entire that it is certain that few such can even be read about, and no trace at all of it can be found among men of today. So many fortuitous circumstances are needed to make it, that it is already something if Fortune can achieve it once in three centuries. There seems to be nothing for which Nature has better prepared us than for fellowship – and Aristotle says that good lawgivers have shown more concern for friendship than for justice. Within a fellowship the peak of perfection consists in friendship; for all forms of it which are forged or fostered by pleasure or profit or by public or private necessity are so much the less beautiful and noble – and therefore so much the less 'friendship' – in that they bring in some purpose, end or fruition other than the friendship itself. Nor do those four ancient species of love conform to it: the natural, the social, the hospitable and the erotic.

From children to fathers it is more a matter of respect; friendship, being fostered by mutual confidences, cannot exist between them because of their excessive inequality; it might also interfere with their natural obligations: for all the secret thoughts of fathers cannot be shared with their children for fear of begetting an unbecoming intimacy; neither can those counsels and admonitions which constitute one of the principal obligations of friendship be offered by children to their fathers. There have been peoples where it was the custom for children to kill their fathers and others for fathers to kill their children to avoid the impediment which each can constitute for the other: one depends naturally on the downfall of the other.

There have been philosophers who held such natural bonds in contempt – witness Aristippus: when he was being pressed about the affection which he owed to his children since they had sprung from him, he began to spit, saying that that sprang from him too, and that we also engender lice and worms. And there was that other one whom Plutarch sought to reconcile with his brother but who retorted: 'He matters no more to me for coming out of the same hole.'

The name of brother is truly a fair one and full of love: that is why La Boëtie and I made a brotherhood of our alliance. But sharing out property or dividing it up, with the wealth of one becoming the poverty of the other, can wondrously melt and weaken the solder binding brothers together. Brothers have to progress and advance by driving along the same path in the same convoy: they needs must frequently bump and jostle against each other. Moreover, why should there be found between them that congruity and affinity which engender true and perfect friendship? Father and son can be of totally different complexions: so can brothers. 'He is my son, he is my kinsman, but he is wild, wicked or daft!' And to the extent that they are loving relationships commanded by the law and the bonds of nature, there is less of our own choice, less 'willing freedom'. Our 'willing freedom' produces nothing more properly its own than affection and loving-friendship. It is not that I have failed to assay all that the other kind can afford, having had the best father who ever was, and the most indulgent even into extreme old age, and coming as I do from a family renowned and exemplary from generation to generation in the matter of brotherly harmony:

> *et ipse*
> *Notus in fratres animi paterni.*

[And myself known for my fatherly concern for my brothers.]*

You cannot compare with friendship the passion men feel for women, even though it is born of our own choice, nor can you put them in the same category. I must admit that the flames of passion –

> *neque enim est dea nescia nostri*
> *Que dulcem curis miscet amaritiem*

[for I am not unacquainted with that goddess who mingles sweet bitterness with love's cares]†–

are more active, sharp and keen. But that fire is a rash one, fickle, fluctuating and variable; it is a feverish fire, subject to attacks and relapses, which only gets hold of a corner of us. The love of friends is a general universal warmth, temperate moreover and smooth, a warmth which is constant and at rest, all gentleness and evenness, having nothing sharp nor keen. What is more, sexual love is but a mad craving for something which escapes us:

> *Come segue la lepre il cacciatore*
> *Al freddo, al caldo, alla montagna, al lito;*
> *Ne piu l'estima poi che presa vede,*
> *Et sol dietro a chi fugge affretta il piede.*

[Like the hunter who chases the hare through heat and cold,

---

* Horace, *Odes*, II, ii, 6–7 (adapted to apply to Montaigne).
† Catullus, *Epigrams*, LXVI, 17–18.

o'er hill and dale, yet, once he has bagged it, he thinks nothing of it; only while it flees away does he pound after it.]*

As soon as it enters the territory of friendship (where wills work together, that is) it languishes and grows faint. To enjoy it is to lose it: its end is in the body and therefore subject to satiety. Friendship on the contrary is enjoyed in proportion to our desire: since it is a matter of the mind, with our souls being purified by practising it, it can spring forth, be nourished and grow only when enjoyed. Far below such perfect friendship those fickle passions also once found a place in me – not to mention in La Boëtie, who confesses to all too many in his verses. And so those two emotions came into me, each one aware of the other but never to be compared, the first maintaining its course in a proud and lofty flight, scornfully watching the other racing along way down below.

As for marriage, apart from being a bargain where only the entrance is free (its duration being fettered and constrained, depending on things outside our will), it is a bargain struck for other purposes; within it you soon have to unsnarl hundreds of extraneous tangled ends, which are enough to break the thread of a living passion and to trouble its course, whereas in friendship there is no traffic or commerce but with itself. In addition, women are in truth not normally capable of responding to such familiarity and mutual confidence as sustain that holy bond of friendship, nor do their souls seem firm

* Ariosto, *Orlando furioso*, X, vii.

enough to withstand the clasp of a knot so lasting and so tightly drawn. And indeed if it were not for that, if it were possible to fashion such a relationship, willing and free, in which not only the souls had this full enjoyment but in which the bodies too shared in the union – where the whole human being was involved – it is certain that the loving-friendship would be more full and more abundant. But there is no example yet of woman attaining to it and by the common agreement of the Ancient schools of philosophy she is excluded from it.

And that alternative licence of the Greeks is rightly abhorrent to our manners; moreover since as they practised it it required a great disparity of age and divergence of favours between the lovers, it did not correspond either to that perfect union and congruity which we are seeking here. '*Quis est enim iste amor amicitiae? Cur neque deformem adolescentem quisquam amat, neque formosum senem?*' [What is this 'friendship-love'? Why does nobody ever fall in love with a youth who is ugly or with a beautiful *old* man?]* For even the portrayal of it by the Academy will not I think belie me when I say this about it: that the original frenzy inspired by Venus' son in the heart of the Lover towards the bloom of a tender youth (in which they allow all the excessive and passionate assaults which an immoderate ardour can produce) was simply based on physical beauty, a false image of generation in the body (for it could not have been based on the

---

* Cicero, *Tusc. disput.*, IV, xxxiii, 70. (In Greek philosophical homosexuality the older man was the Lover; the younger, the Beloved, showed admiration, or gratitude for instruction.)

mind, which had yet to show itself, which was even then being born, too young to sprout); that if so mad a passion took hold of a base mind the means of pursuing it were riches, presents, favouritism in advancement to high office and such other base traffickings which the Academy condemned; if it lighted on a more noble mind its inducements were likewise more noble: instruction in philosophy; lessons teaching reverence for religion, obedience to the law and dying for the good of one's country; examples of valour, wisdom, justice, with the Lover striving to make himself worthy of acceptance by the graciousness and beauty of his soul (that of his body having long since faded) and hoping by this mental alliance to strike a more firm and durable match. When this suit produced its results – in due season (for while they did not require the Lover to devote time and discretion to this undertaking they strictly required it of the Beloved, since he had to reach a judgement about a kind of beauty which is internal, difficult to recognize and concealed from discovery) – there was then born in that Beloved the desire mentally to conceive through the medium of the beauty of the mind. For him this beauty was pre-eminent: that of the body, secondary and contingent – quite the opposite from the Lover. For this reason they held the Beloved in higher esteem and proved that the gods do so too; they severely rebuked the poet Aeschylus for having given, in the love of Achilles and Patroclus, the role of the Lover to Achilles, who was the fairest of all the Greeks, in the first verdure of unbearded youth.

Once this general communion had been established,

with the more worthy aspect of it fulfilling its duties and predominating, they said that it produced fruits useful for private and public life; that it was the strength of those countries where it was the accepted custom and the main defence of right conduct and freedom – witness the loves of Hermodius and Aristogiton. That is why they call it sacred and divine. By their reckoning only the violence of tyrants and the baseness of the people are opposed to it. Yet when all is said and done the only point we can concede to the Academy is that it was a love-affair which ended in friendship – which conforms well enough to the Stoic definition of love: '*Amorem conatum esse amicitiae faciendae ex pulchritudinis specie.*' [Love is the striving to establish friendship on the external signs of beauty.]*

I now return to a kind of love more equable and more equitable: '*Omnino amicitiae, corroboratis jam confirmatisque ingeniis et aetatibus, judicandae sunt.*' [Such only are to be considered friendships in which characters have been confirmed and strengthened with age.]†

Moreover what we normally call friends and friendships are no more than acquaintances and familiar relationships bound by some chance or some suitability, by means of which our souls support each other. In the friendship which I am talking about, souls are mingled and confounded in so universal a blending that they efface the seam which joins them together so that it cannot be found. If you press me to say why I loved him, I feel that it cannot be expressed except by replying:

---

* Cicero, *Tusc. disput.*, IV, xxiv, 71.   † Cicero, *De amicitia*, XX, 74.

'Because it was him: because it was me.' Mediating this union there was, beyond all my reasoning, beyond all that I can say specifically about it, some inexplicable force of destiny.

We were seeking each other before we set eyes on each other – both because of the reports we each had heard (which made a more violent assault on our emotions than was reasonable from what they had said, and, I believe, because of some decree of Heaven: we embraced each other by repute, and, at our first meeting, which chanced to be at a great crowded town-festival, we discovered ourselves to be so seized by each other, so known to each other and so bound together that from then on none was so close as each was to the other. He wrote an excellent Latin *Satire*, which has been published, by which he defends and explains the suddenness of our relationship which so quickly reached perfection. Having so short a period to last, having begun so late (for we were both grown men – he more than a few years older than I) – it had no time to waste on following the pattern of those slacker ordinary friendships which require so much prudent foresight in long preliminary acquaintance. This friendship has had no ideal to follow other than itself; no comparison but with itself. There is no one particular consideration – nor two nor three nor four nor a thousand of them – but rather some inexplicable quintessence of them all mixed up together which, having captured my will, brought it to plunge into his and lose itself and which, having captured his will, brought it to plunge and lose itself in mine with an equal hunger and emulation. I say 'lose itself' in very truth; we kept nothing back for ourselves: nothing was his or mine.

In the presence of the Roman Consuls (who, after the condemnation of Tiberius Gracchus were prosecuting those who had been in his confidence) Laelius eventually asked Caius Blosius, the closest friend of Gracchus, how much he would have done for him. He replied: 'Anything.' – 'What, anything?' Laelius continued: 'And what if he had ordered you to set fire to our temples?' – 'He would never have asked me to,' retorted Blosius. 'But supposing he had,' Laelius added. 'Then I would have obeyed,' he replied.* Now if he really were so perfect a friend of Gracchus as history asserts, he had no business provoking the Consuls with that last rash assertion and ought never to have abandoned the certainty he had of the wishes of Gracchus. But those who condemn his reply as seditious do not fully understand the mystery of friendship and fail to accept the premiss that he had Gracchus' intentions in the pocket of his sleeve, both by his influence and by his knowledge. They were more friends than citizens; friends, more than friends or foes of their country or friends of ambition and civil strife. Having completely committed themselves to each other, they each completely held the reins of each other's desires; grant that this pair were guided by virtue and led by reason (without which it is impossible to harness them together) Blosius' reply is what it should have been. If their actions broke the traces, then they were, by my measure, neither friends of each other nor friends

* Cicero, *De amicitia*, XI, 33–9.

of themselves. Moreover that reply sounds no different than mine would be, if I were interrogated thus: 'If your will commanded you to kill your daughter would you kill her?' and I said that I would. For that is no witness that I would consent to do so, because I do not doubt what my will is, any more than I doubt the will of such a friend. All the arguments in the world have no power to dislodge me from the certainty which I have of the intentions and decisions of my friend. Not one of his actions could be set before me – no matter what it looked like – without my immediately discovering its motive. Our souls were yoked together in such unity, and contemplated each other with so ardent an affection, and with the same affection revealed each to each other right down to the very entrails, that not only did I know his mind as well as I knew my own but I would have entrusted myself to him with greater assurance than to myself.

Let nobody place those other common friendships in the same rank as this. I know about them – the most perfect of their kind – as well as anyone else, but I would advise you not to confound their rules: you would deceive yourself. In those other friendships you must proceed with wisdom and caution, keeping the reins in your hand: the bond is not so well tied that there is no reason to doubt it. 'Love a friend,' said Chilo, 'as though some day you must hate him: hate him, as though you must love him'.* That precept which is so detestable in

---

* Chilo's chilling judgement was normally attributed to Bias, one of the Seven Sages of Greece.

that sovereign master-friendship is salutary in the practice of friendships which are common and customary, in relation to which you must employ that saying which Aristotle often repeated: 'O my friends, there is no friend!'*

In this noble relationship, the services and good turns which foster those other friendships do not even merit being taken into account: that is because of the total interfusion of our wills. For just as the friendly love I feel for myself is not increased – no matter what the Stoics may say – by any help I give myself in my need, and just as I feel no gratitude for any good turn I do to myself: so too the union of such friends, being truly perfect, leads them to lose any awareness of such services, to hate and to drive out from between them all terms of division and difference, such as good turn, duty, gratitude, request, thanks and the like. Everything is genuinely common to them both: their wills, goods, wives, children, honour and lives; their correspondence is that of one soul in bodies twain, according to that most apt definition of Aristotle's,† so they can neither lend nor give anything to each other. That is why those who make laws forbid gifts between husband and wife, so as to honour marriage with some imagined resemblance to that holy bond, wishing to infer by it that everything must belong to them both, so that there is nothing to divide or to split up between them. In the kind of friendship I am talking about, if it were possible for one

* Erasmus, *Apophthegmata*, VII, *Aristoteles Stagirites*, XXVIII.
† Erasmus, ibid., VII, *Aristoteles Stagirites*, XIX.

to give to the other it is the one who received the benefaction who would lay an obligation on his companion. For each of them, more than anything else, is seeking the good of the other, so that the one who furnishes the means and the occasion is in fact the more generous, since he gives his friend the joy of performing for him what he most desires. When Diogenes the philosopher was short of money he did not say that he would ask his friends to give him some but to give him some back!* And to show how this happens in practice I will cite an example – a unique one – from Antiquity.

Eudamidas, a Corinthian, had two friends: Charixenus, a Sicyonian, and Aretheus, also a Corinthian. As he happened to die in poverty, his two friends being rich, he made the following testament: 'To Aretheus I bequeath that he look after my mother and maintain her in her old age; to Charixenus, that he see that my daughter be married, providing her with the largest dowry he can; and if one of them should chance to die I appoint the survivor to substitute for him.' Those who first saw his will laughed at it; but, when those heirs learned of it, they accepted it with a unique joy. One of them, Charixenus, did die five days later; the possibility of substitution was thus opened in favour of Aretheus, and he looked after the mother with much care; then, of five hundred weight of silver in his possession, he gave two and a half for the marriage of his only daughter and two and a half for the daughter of

* Erasmus, ibid., III, *Diogenes Cynicus*, LXXXII.

Eudamidas, celebrating their weddings on the same day.*

This example is a most full one, save for one circumstance: there was more than one friend. For the perfect friendship which I am talking about is indivisible: each gives himself so entirely to his friend that he has nothing left to share with another: on the contrary, he grieves that he is not two-fold, three-fold or four-fold and that he does not have several souls, several wills, so that he could give them all to the one he loves.

Common friendships can be shared. In one friend one can love beauty; in another, affability; in another, generosity; in another, a fatherly affection; in another, a brotherly one; and so on. But in this friendship love takes possession of the soul and reigns there with full sovereign sway: that cannot possibly be duplicated. If two friends asked you to help them at the same time, which of them would you dash to? If they asked for conflicting favours, who would have the priority? If one entrusted to your silence something which it was useful for the other to know, how would you get out of that? The unique, highest friendship loosens all other bonds. That secret which I have sworn to reveal to no other, I can reveal without perjury to him who is not another: he *is* me. It is a great enough miracle for oneself to be re-doubled: they do not realize how high a one it is when they talk of its being tripled. The uttermost cannot be matched. If anyone suggests that I can love each of two friends as much as the other, and that they can love

* From Lucian of Samosata, *Toxaris, or, On friendship*, XXII.

each other and love me as much as I love them, he is turning into a plural, into a confraternity, that which is the most 'one', the most bound into one. One single example of it is moreover the rarest thing to find in the world.

The rest of that story conforms well what I was saying: for Eudamidas bestows a grace and favour on his friends when he makes use of them in his necessity. He left them heirs to his own generosity, which consists in putting into their hands the means of doing him good. And there is no doubt that the force of loving-friendship is more richly displayed in what he did than in what Aretheus did. To sum up, these are deeds which surpass the imagination of anyone who has not tasted them; they make me wondrously honour the reply of that young soldier when Cyrus inquired of him how much he would take for a horse which had enabled him to win the prize in the races: 'Would he sell it for a kingdom?' – 'No, indeed, Sire; but I would willingly give it away to gain a friend, if I could find a man worthy of such an alliance.'* Not badly put, that, 'If I could find'; for you can easily find men fit for a superficial acquaintanceship. But for our kind, in which we are dealing with the innermost recesses of our minds with no reservations, it is certain that all of our motives must be pure and sure to perfection.

In those alliances which only get hold of us by one end, we need simply to provide against such flaws as specifically affect that end. It cannot matter to me what

---

* Xenophon, *Cyropaedia*, VIII, iii, 270.

the religion of my doctor or my lawyer is: that consideration has nothing in common with the friendly services which they owe to me. And in such commerce as arises at home with my servants I act the same way: I make few inquiries about the chastity of my footman: I want to know if he is hard-working; I am less concerned by a mule-driver who gambles than by one who is an idiot, or by a cook who swears than by one who is incompetent. It is not my concern to tell the world how to behave (plenty of others do that) but how I behave in it:

> *Mihi sic usus est; tibi, ut opus est facto, face.*
> [This is what I do: do what serves you.]*

For the intimate companionship of my table I choose the agreeable not the wise; in my bed, beauty comes before virtue; in social conversation, ability – even without integrity. And so on.

Just as that philosopher† playing with his children and riding astride a hobby-horse told the man who surprised him at it not to make comments before he had children of his own, judging that the emotions which would then arise in his soul would make him a good judge of such behaviour: so too I could wish that I were speaking to people who had assayed what I am talking about; but realizing how far removed from common practice is such a friendship – and how rare it is – I do not expect to find one good judge of it. For the very writings which

* Terence, *Heautontimorumenos*, I, i, 28.
† Agesilaus (Cf. Erasmus, *Apophthegmata*, I, *Agesilaus*, LXVIII).

Antiquity have left us on this subject seem weak to me compared to what I feel. In this case the very precepts of philosophy are surpassed by the results:

> *Nil ego contulerim jucundo sanus amico.*
> [Whilst I am in my right mind, there is nothing I will compare with a delightful friend.]*

In Antiquity Menander pronounced a man to be happy if he had merely encountered the shadow of a friend.† He was certainly right to say so, especially if he had actually tasted friendship. For in truth if I compare all the rest of my life – although by the grace of God I have lived it sweetly and easily, exempt (save for the death of such a friend) from grievous affliction in full tranquillity of mind, contenting myself with the natural endowments which I was born with and not going about looking for others – if I compare it, I say, to those four years which it was vouchsafed to me to enjoy in the sweet companionship and fellowship of a man like that, it is but smoke and ashes, a night dark and dreary.

Since that day when I lost him,

> *quem semper acerbum,*
> *Semper honoratum (sic, Dii, voluistis) habebo,*
> [which I shall ever hold bitter to me, though always honour (since the gods ordained it so),]‡

* Horace, *Satires*, I, v, 44.
† Plutarch (tr. Amyot), *De l'amitié fraternelle*, 82C–D.
‡ Virgil, *Aeneid*, V, 49–50.

I merely drag wearily on. The very pleasures which are proffered me do not console me: they redouble my sorrow at his loss. In everything we were halves: I feel I am stealing his share from him:

> *Nec fas esse ulla me voluptate hic frui*
> *Decrevi, tantisper dum ille abest meus particeps.*

[Nor is it right for me to enjoy pleasures, I decided, while he who shared things with me is absent from me.]*

I was already so used and accustomed to being, in everything, one of two, that I now feel I am no more than a half:

> *Illam meae si partem animae tulit*
> *Maturior vis, quid moror altera,*
> *Nec charus aeque, nec superstes*
> *Integer? Ille dies utramque*
> *Duxit ruinam.*

[Since an untimely blow has borne away a part of my soul, why do I still linger on less dear, only partly surviving? That day was the downfall of us both.]†

There is no deed nor thought in which I do not miss him – as he would have missed me; for just as he infinitely surpassed me in ability and virtue so did he do so in the offices of friendship:

---

* Terence, *Heautontimorumenos*, I, 1, 97–8.
† Horace, *Odes*, II, xvii, 5–9.

Quis desiderio sit pudor aut modus
Tam chari capitis? . . .
   O misero frater adempte mihi!
Omnia tecum una perierunt gaudia nostra,
   Quae tuus in vita dulcis alebat amor.
Tu mea, tu moriens fregisti commoda, frater;
   Tecum una tota est nostra sepulta anima,
Cujus ego interitu tota de mente fugavi
   Haec studia atque omnes delicias animi.
Alloquar? audiero nunquam tua verba loquentem?
   Nunquam ego te, vita frater amabilior,
Aspiciam posthac? At certe semper amabo.

[What shame or limit should there be to grief for one so dear?
. . . How wretched I am, having lost such a brother! With you
died all our joys, which your sweet love fostered when you
were alive. You, brother, have destroyed my happiness by
your death: all my soul is buried with you. Because of your
loss I have chased all thoughts from my mind and all pleasures
from my soul . . . Shall I never speak to you, never hear you
talking of what you have done? Shall I never see you again,
my brother, dearer than life itself? But certainly I shall love
you always.]*

Let us hear a while this sixteen-year-old boy.

Having discovered that this work of his has since been
published to an evil end by those who seek to disturb
and change the state of our national polity without
worrying whether they will make it better, and that they
have set it among works of their own kidney, I have

* Catullus, LXVIII, 20f.; LXV, 9 f. (adapted).

gone back on my decision to place it here. And so that the author's reputation should not be harmed among those who cannot know his opinions or his actions, I tell them that this subject was treated by him in his childhood purely as an exercise; it is a commonplace theme, pawed over in hundreds and hundreds of books. I have no doubt that he believed what he wrote, for he was too conscientious to tell untruths even in a light-hearted work. And I know, moreover, that if he had had the choice he would rather have been born in Venice than in Sarlat. Rightly so. But he had another maxim supremely imprinted upon his soul: to obey, and most scrupulously submit to, the laws under which he was born. There never was a better citizen, one more devoted to his country's peace or more opposed to the disturbances and novelties of his time. He would have used his abilities to snuff them out, not to provide materials to stir them up. The mould of his mind was cast on the model of centuries different from ours.

So instead of that serious work I will substitute another one, more gallant and more playful, which he wrote in the same season of his life.

2

That it is madness to judge the true and the false from our own capacities

It is not perhaps without good reason that we attribute to simple-mindedness a readiness to believe anything and to ignorance the readiness to be convinced, for I think I was once taught that a belief is like an impression stamped on our soul: the softer and less resisting the soul, the easier it is to print anything on it: '*Ut necesse est lancem in libra ponderibus impositis deprimi, sic animum perspicuis cedere.*' ['For just as a weight placed on a balance must weigh it down, so the mind must yield to clear evidence.']* The more empty a soul is and the less furnished with counterweights, the more easily its balance will be swayed under the force of its first convictions. That is why children, the common people, women and the sick are more readily led by the nose.

On the other hand there is a silly arrogance in continuing to disdain something and to condemn it as false just because it seems unlikely to us. That is a common vice among those who think their capacities are above the ordinary.

I used to do that once: if I heard tell of ghosts walking

* Cicero, *Academica*, II, ii, 127.

or of prophecies, enchantments, sorcery, or some other tale which I could not get my teeth into –

Somnia, terrores magicos, miracula, sagas,
Nocturnos lemures portentaque Thessala

[Dreams, magic terrors, miracles, witches, nocturnal visits from the dead or spells from Thessaly]*

– I used to feel sorry for the wretched folk who were taken in by such madness. Now I find that I was at least as much to be pitied as they were. It is not that experience has subsequently shown me anything going beyond my original beliefs (nor is it from any lack of curiosity on my part), but reason has taught me that, if you condemn in this way anything whatever as definitely false and quite impossible, you are claiming to know the frontiers and bounds of the will of God and the power of Nature our Mother; it taught me also that there is nothing in the whole world madder than bringing matters down to the measure of our own capacities and potentialities.

How many of the things which constantly come into our purview must be deemed monstrous or miraculous if we apply such terms to anything which outstrips our reason! If we consider that we have to grope through a fog even to understand the very things we hold in our hands, then we will certainly find that it is not knowledge but habit which takes away their strangeness;

* Horace, *Epistles*, II, ii, 208–9.

> *jam nemo, fessus satiate vivendi,*
> *Suspicere in coeli dignatur lucida templa;*

[Already now, tired and satiated with life, nobody bothers to gaze up at the shining temples of the heavens:]

such things, if they were newly presented to us, would seem as unbelievable as any others;

> *si nunc primum mortalibus adsint*
> *Ex improviso, ceu sint objecta repente,*
> *Nil magis his rebus poterat mirabile dici,*
> *Aut minus ante quod auderent fore credere gentes.*

[supposing that now, for the first time, they were suddenly shown to mortal men: nothing could be called more miraculous; such things the nations would not have dared to believe.]*

He who had never actually seen a river, the first time he did so took it for the ocean, since we think that the biggest things that we know represent the limits of what Nature can produce in that species.

> *Scilicet et fluvius, qui non est maximus, eii est*
> *Qui non ante aliquem majorem vidit, et ingens*
> *Arbor homoque videtur; et omnia de genere omni*
> *Maxima quae vidit quisque, haec ingentia fingit.*

[Just as a river may not be all that big, but seems huge to a man who has never seen a bigger one, so, too, for the biggest tree or biggest man; and the biggest thing of any kind which we know is considered huge by us.]

* Lucretius, II, 1037–8; 1032–5.

'*Consuetudine oculorum assuescunt animi, neque admirantur, neque requirunt rationes earum rerum quas semper vident.*' [When we grow used to seeing anything it accustoms our minds to it and we cease to be astonished by it; we never seek the causes of things like that.]* What makes us seek the cause of anything is not size but novelty.

We ought to judge the infinite power of Nature with more reverence and a greater recognition of our own ignorance and weakness. How many improbable things there are which have been testified to by people worthy of our trust: if we cannot be convinced we should at least remain in suspense. To condemn them as impossible is to be rashly presumptuous, boasting that we know the limits of the possible. If we understood the difference between what is impossible and what is unusual, or between what is against the order of the course of Nature and what is against the common opinion of mankind, then the way to observe that rule laid down by Chilo, *Nothing to excess*, would be, Not to believe too rashly: not to disbelieve too easily.

When we read in Froissart that the Comte de Foix knew the following morning in Béarn of the defeat of King John of Castille at Juberoth, and when we read of the means he is alleged to have used, we can laugh at that; we can laugh too when our annals tell how Pope Honorius, on the very same day that King Philip-Augustus died at Mante, celebrated a public requiem for him and ordered the same to be done throughout Italy,

---

* Lucretius, VI, 674–7; Cicero, *De natura deorum*, II, XXXVIII, 96.

for the authority of such witnesses is not high enough to rein us back.

But wait. When Plutarch (leaving aside the many examples which he alleges from Antiquity) says that he himself knows quite definitely that, at the time of Domitian, news of the battle lost by Antony several days' journey away in Germany was publicly announced in Rome and spread through all the world on the very day that it was lost; and when Caesar maintains that it was often the case that news of an event actually anticipated the event itself: are we supposed to say that they were simple people who merely followed the mob and who let themselves be deceived because they saw things less clearly than we do!*

Can there be anything more delicate, clear-cut and lively than the judgement of Pliny when he pleases to exercise it? Is there anything further from triviality? (I am not discussing his outstanding erudition; I put less store by that: but in which of those two qualities are we supposed to surpass him?) And yet every little schoolboy convicts him of lying and lectures him about the march of Nature's handiwork.

When we read in Bouchet about miracles associated with the relics of Saint Hilary we can shrug it off: his right to be believed is not great enough to take away our freedom to challenge him. But to go on from there and condemn all similar accounts seems to me to be impudent in the extreme. Such a great saint as Augustine

---

* Plutarch, *Life of Paulus Aemilius*. The reference to Caesar is puzzling.

swears that he saw:* a blind child restored to sight by
the relics of Saint Gervaise and Saint Protasius at Milan;
a woman in Carthage cured of a cancer by the sign of
the cross made by a woman who had just been baptised;
his close friend Hesperius driving off devils (who were
infesting his house) by using a little soil taken from the
sepulchre of our Lord, and that same soil, borne into the
Church, suddenly curing a paralytic; a woman who,
having touched the reliquary of Saint Stephen with a
posy of flowers during a procession, rubbed her eyes
with them afterwards and recovered her sight which she
had recently lost – as well as several other miracles which
occurred in his presence. What are we to accuse him of
– him and the two holy bishops, Aurelius and Maximinus,
whom he calls on as witnesses? Is it of ignorance, simple-
mindedness, credulity, deliberate deception or impos-
ture? Is there any man in our century so impudent as to
think he can be compared with them for virtue, piety,
scholarship, judgement and ability? *'Qui, ut rationem nul-
lam afferent, ipsa authoritate me frangerent.'* [Why, even if
they gave no reasons, they would convince me by their
very authority.]†

Apart from the absurd rashness which it entails, there
is a dangerous boldness of great consequence in despising
whatever we cannot understand. For as soon as you
have established the frontiers of truth and error with
that fine brain of yours and then discover that you must
of necessity believe some things even stranger than the

* St Augustine, *City of God*, XII, viii.
† Cicero, *Tusc. disput.*, I, xxi, 49, adapted.

ones which you reject, you are already forced to abandon these frontiers.

Now it seems to me that what brings as much disorder as anything into our consciences during our current religious strife is the way Catholics are prepared to treat some of their beliefs as expendable. They believe they are being moderate and well-informed when they surrender to their enemies some of the articles of faith which are in dispute. But, apart from the fact that they cannot see what an advantage you give to an adversary when you begin to yield ground and beat a retreat, or how much that excites him to follow up his attack, the very articles which they select as being less weighty are sometimes extremely important ones.

We must either totally submit to the authority of our ecclesiastical polity or else totally release ourselves from it. It is not for us to decide what degree of obedience we owe to it.

Moreover I can say that for having assayed it; in the past I made use of that freedom of personal choice and private selection in order to neglect certain details in the observances of our Church because they seemed to be rather odd or rather empty; then, when I came to tell some learned men about it, I discovered that those very practices were based on massive and absolutely solid foundations, and that it is only our ignorance and animal-stupidity which make us treat them with less reverence than all the rest.

Why cannot we remember all the contradictions which we feel within our own judgement, and how many things which were articles of belief for us yesterday are fables for us today?

Vainglory and curiosity are the twin scourges of our souls. The former makes us stick our noses into every-thing: the latter forbids us to leave anything unresolved or undecided.

3

On the art of conversation

It is a custom of our justice to punish some as a warning
to others. For to punish them for *having done* wrong
would, as Plato says, be stupid: what is done cannot be
undone. The intention is to stop them from repeating
the same mistake or to make others avoid their error.*
We do not improve the man we hang: we improve
others by him. I do the same. My defects are becoming
natural and incorrigible, but as fine gentlemen serve the
public as models to follow I may serve a turn as a model
to avoid:

> *Nonne vides Albi ut male vivat filius, utque*
> *Barrus inops? magnum documentum, ne patriam rem*
> *Perdere quis velit*

[You can see, can't you, how wretchedly Albus' son is living
and how poor Barrus is? An excellent lesson in not squandering
your inheritance.]†

The act of publishing and indicting my imperfections
may teach someone how to fear them. (The talents
which I most esteem in myself derive more honour from

* Plato, *Laws*, XI, 934 A–B.   † Horace, *Satires*, I, iv, 109–11.

indicting me than praising me.) That is why I so often
return to it and linger over it. Yet, when all has been said,
you never talk about yourself without loss: condemn
yourself and you are always believed: praise yourself
and you never are.

There may be others of my complexion who learn
better by counter-example than by example, by
eschewing not pursuing. That was the sort of instruction
which the Elder Cato was thinking of when he said that
the wise have more to learn from the fools than the fools
from the wise;* as also that lyre-player in antiquity who,
Pausanias says, used to require his students to go and
listen to some performer who lived across the street
so that they would learn to loathe discords and faulty
rhythms.† My horror of cruelty thrusts me deeper into
clemency than any example of clemency ever could draw
me. A good equerry does not make me sit up straight in
the saddle as much as the sight of a lawyer or a Venetian
out riding, and a bad use of language corrects my own
better than a good one. Every day I am warned and
counselled by the stupid deportment of someone. What
hits you affects you and wakes you up more than what
pleases you. We can only improve ourselves in times
such as these by walking backwards, by discord not by
harmony, by being different not by being like. Having
myself learned little from good examples I use the bad
ones, the text of which is routine. I strove to be as
agreeable as others were seen to be boring; as firm as

---

* Erasmus, *Apophthegmata*, V, *Cato Senior*, XXXIX.
† Anecdote not traced. Perhaps a confusion with the practice of the
ancient musician Timotheus of Miletus. Cf. Quintilian, II, iii, 3.

others were flabby; as gentle as others were sharp. But I was setting myself unattainable standards.

To my taste the most fruitful and most natural exercise of our minds is conversation. I find the practice of it the most delightful activity in our lives. That is why, if I were now obliged to make the choice, I think I would rather lose my sight than my powers of speech or hearing. In their academies the Athenians, and even more the Romans, maintained this exercise in great honour. In our own times the Italians retain some vestiges of it – greatly to their benefit, as can be seen from a comparison of their intelligence and ours. Studying books has a languid feeble motion, whereas conversation provides teaching and exercise all at once. If I am sparring with a strong and solid opponent he will attack me on the flanks, stick his lance in me right and left; his ideas send mine soaring. Rivalry, competitiveness and glory will drive me and raise me above my own level. In conversation the most painful quality is perfect harmony.

Just as our mind is strengthened by contact with vigorous and well-ordered minds, so too it is impossible to overstate how much it loses and deteriorates by the continuous commerce and contact we have with mean and ailing ones. No infection is as contagious as that is. I know by experience what that costs by the ell. I love arguing and discussing, but with only a few men and for my own sake: for to serve as a spectacle to the great and indulge in a parade of your wits and your verbiage is, I consider, an unbecoming trade for an honourable gentleman.

Stupidity is a bad quality: but to be unable to put up

with it, to be vexed and ground down by it (as happens to me) is another, hardly worse in its unmannerliness than stupidity. And that is what at present I wish to condemn in myself.

I embark upon discussion and argument with great ease and liberty. Since opinions do not find in me a ready soil to thrust and spread their roots into, no premise shocks me, no belief hurts me, no matter how opposite to my own they may be. There is no idea so frivolous or odd which does not appear to me to be fittingly produced by the mind of man. Those of us who deprive our judgement of the right to pass sentence look gently on strange opinions; we may not lend them our approbation but we do readily lend them our ears. When one scale in the balance is quite empty I will let the other be swayed by an old woman's dreams: so it seems pardonable if I choose the odd number rather than the even, or Thursday rather than Friday; if I prefer to be twelfth or fourteenth at table rather than thirteenth; if I prefer on my travels to see a hare skirting my path rather than crossing it, and offer my left foot to be booted before the right. All such lunacies (which are believed among us) at least deserve to be heard. For me they only outweigh an empty scale, but outweigh it they do. Similarly the weight of popular and unfounded opinions has a natural existence which is more than nothing. A man who will not go that far perhaps avoids the vice of superstition by falling into the vice of stubbornness.

So contradictory judgements neither offend me nor irritate me: they merely wake me up and provide me with exercise. We avoid being corrected: we ought to come forward and accept it, especially when it comes from conversation not a lecture. Whenever we meet opposition, we do not look to see if it is just but how we can get out of it, rightly or wrongly. Instead of welcoming arms we stretch out our claws. I can put up with being roughly handled by my friends: 'You are an idiot! You are raving!' Among gentlemen I like people to express themselves heartily, their words following wherever their thoughts lead. We ought to toughen and fortify our ears against being seduced by the sound of polite words. I like a strong, intimate, manly fellowship, the kind of friendship which rejoices in sharp vigorous exchanges just as love rejoices in bites and scratches which draw blood. It is not strong enough nor magnanimous enough if it is not argumentative, if all is politeness and art; if it is afraid of clashes and walks hobbled. '*Neque enim disputari sine reprehensione potest.*' [It is impossible to debate without refuting.]*

When I am contradicted it arouses my attention not my wrath. I move towards the man who contradicts me: he is instructing me. The cause of truth ought to be common to us both. – What will his answer be? The passion of anger has already wounded his judgement. Turbulence has seized it before reason can. – It would be a useful idea if we had to wager on the deciding of our quarrels, useful if there were a material sign of our defeats so that we could keep tally on them and my manservant say: 'Last year your ignorance and stubborn-

---

* Cicero, *De finibus*, I, viii, 28 (Torquatus defending Epicurus' style of conversation).

ness cost you one hundred crowns on twenty occasions.'

I welcome truth, I fondle it, in whosesoever hand I find it; I surrender to it cheerfully, welcoming it with my vanquished arms as soon as I see it approaching from afar. And provided that they do not set about it with too imperious and schoolmasterish a frown I will put my shoulder to the wheel to help along the criticisms that people make of my writings: I have often made changes more for reasons of politeness than to effect reasonable corrections, preferring to please and encourage people's freedom to criticize me by my readiness to give way – yes, even when it cost me something. Yet it is difficult to attract men to do that in our days. They have no stomach for correcting because they have no stomach for suffering correction, always dissembling when talking in each other's presence.

I take such great pleasure in being judged and known that it is virtually indifferent to me which of the two forms it takes. My thought so often contradicts and condemns itself that it is all one to me if someone else does so, seeing that I give to his refutation only such authority as I please. But I fall out with anyone who is too high-handed, like one man I know who laments the fact that he gave you advice if you do not accept it and takes it as an insult if you shy at following it.

Socrates always laughingly welcomed contradictions made to his arguments. It could be said that since his arguments were the stronger the advantage would always fall to him and that he welcomed them as matter for fresh triumphs: but we, on the contrary, find that there is nothing which makes us more susceptible than convictions about our own surpassing excellence, our contempt for our adversary, and about its being reasonable for the weaker to be willing to accept refutations which set him back on his feet and redress him.

I do truly seek to frequent those who manhandle me rather than those who are afraid of me. It is a bland and harmful pleasure to have to deal with people who admire us and defer to us. Antisthenes commanded his sons never to give thanks or show gratitude to anyone who praised them.* I feel far prouder of the victory I win over myself when I make myself give way beneath my adversary's powers of reason in the heat of battle than I ever feel gratified by the victory I win over him through his weakness. In short I admit and acknowledge any attacks, no matter how feeble, if they are made directly, but I am all too impatient of attacks which are not made in due form. I care little about what we are discussing; all opinions are the same to me and it is all but indifferent to me which proposition emerges victorious. I can go on peacefully arguing all day if the debate is conducted with due order. It is not so much forceful and subtle argument that I want as order – the kind of order which can be found every day in disputes among shepherds and shop-assistants yet never among us. If they go astray it is in lack of courtesy. So do we. But their stormy intolerance does not make them stray far from their theme: their arguments keep on course. They interrupt each other. They jostle, but at least get the gist. To answer the point is, in my judgement, to answer very

---

* Plutarch (tr. Amyot), *De la mauvaise honte*, 81 B.

well. But when the discussion becomes turbulent and lacks order, I quit the subject-matter and cling irritably and injudiciously to the form, dashing into a style of debate which is stubborn, ill-willed and imperious, one which I have to blush for later.

It is impossible to argue in good faith with a fool. Not only my judgement is corrupted at the hands of so violent a master, so is my sense of right and wrong. Our quarrels ought to be outlawed and punished as are other verbal crimes. Since they are always ruled and governed by anger, what vices do they not awaken and pile up on each other? First we feel enmity for the arguments and then for the men. In debating we are taught merely how to refute arguments; the result of each side's refuting the other is that the fruit of our debates is the destruction and annihilation of the truth. That is why Plato in his *Republic* prohibits that exercise to ill-endowed minds not suited to it.*

You are in quest of what *is*. Why on earth do you set out to walk that road with a man who has neither pace nor style? We do no wrong to the subject-matter if we depart from it in order to examine the way to treat it – I do not mean a scholastic donnish way, I mean a natural way, based on a healthy intellect. But what happens in the end? One goes east and the other west; they lose the fundamental point in the confusion of a mass of incidentals. After a tempestuous hour they no longer know what they are looking for. One man is beside the bull's eye, the other too high, the other too low. One

* Plato, *Republic*, 539 A–C.

fastens on a word or a comparison; another no longer sees his opponent's arguments, being too caught up in his own train of thought: he is thinking of pursuing his own argument not yours. Another, realizing he is too weak in the loins, is afraid of everything, denies everything and, from the outset, muddles and confuses the argument, or else, at the climax of the debate he falls into a rebellious total silence, affecting, out of morose ignorance, a haughty disdain or an absurdly modest desire to avoid contention. Yet another does not care how much he drops his own guard provided that he can hit you. Another counts every word and believes they are as weighty as reasons. This man merely exploits the superior power of his voice and lungs. And then there is the man who sums up against himself; and the other who deafens you with useless introductions and digressions. Another is armed with pure insults and picks a groundless 'German quarrel' so as to free himself from the company and conversation of a mind which presses hard on his own.

Lastly, there is the man who cannot see reason but holds you under siege within a hedge of dialectical conclusions and logical formulae. Who can avoid beginning to distrust our professional skills and doubt whether we can extract from them any solid profit of practical use in life when he reflects on the use we put them to? '*Nihil sanantibus litteris.*' [Such erudition as has no power to heal.]* Has anyone ever acquired intelligence through

---

* Seneca, *Epist. moral.*, LIX, 15; then, Cicero, *De finibus*, I, xix, 63, criticizing Epicurean logic.

logic? Where are her beautiful promises? *'Nec ad melius
vivendum nec ad commodius disserendum.'* [She teaches
neither how to live a better life nor how to argue properly.] Is there more of a hotchpotch in the cackle of
fishwives than in the public disputations of men who
profess logic? I would prefer a son of mine to learn to
talk in the tavern rather than in our university yap-shops.

Take an arts don; converse with him. Why is he
incapable of making us feel the excellence of his 'arts'
and of throwing the women, and us ignoramuses, into
ecstasies of admiration at the solidity of his arguments
and the beauty of his ordered rhetoric? Why cannot he
overmaster us and sway us at his will? Why does a man
with his superior mastery of matter and style intermingle
his sharp thrusts with insults, indiscriminate arguments
and rage? Let him remove his academic hood, his gown
and his Latin; let him stop battering our ears with raw
chunks of pure Aristotle; why, you would take him for
one of us – or worse. The involved linguistic convol-
utions with which they confound us remind me of con-
juring tricks: their sleight-of-hand has compelling force
over our senses but it in no wise shakes our convictions.
Apart from such jugglery they achieve nothing but what
is base and ordinary. They may be more learned but
they are no less absurd.

I like and honour erudition as much as those who
have it. When used properly it is the most noble and
powerful acquisition of Man. But in the kind of men
(and their number is infinite) who make it the base and
foundation of their worth and achievement, who quit
their understanding for their memory, *'sub aliena umbra*

latentes' [hiding behind other men's shadows],* and can do nothing except by book, I loathe (dare I say it?) a little more than I loathe stupidity.

In my part of the country and during my own lifetime school-learning has brought amendment of purse but rarely amendment of soul. If the souls it meets are already obtuse, as a raw and undigested mass it clogs and suffocates them; if they are unfettered, it tends to purge them, strip them of impurities and volatilize them into vacuity. Erudition is a thing the quality of which is neither good nor bad, almost: it is a most useful adjunct to a well-endowed soul: to any other it is baleful and harmful; or rather, it is a thing which, in use, has great value, but it will not allow itself to be acquired at a base price: in one hand it is a royal sceptre, in another, a fool's bauble.

But to get on: what greater victory do you want than to teach your enemy that he cannot stand up to you? Get the better of him by your argument and the winner is the truth; do so by your order and style, then you are the winner!

I am persuaded that, in both Plato and Xenophon, Socrates debates more for the debater's than for debating's sake; more to teach Euthydemus and Protagoras their own absurdity than the absurdity of their sophists' art. He seizes hold of the first subject which comes to hand, as a man who has a more useful aim than to throw light on his subject as such: namely, to enlighten the minds which he accepts to train and to exercise. The

* Seneca, *Epist. moral.*, XXXIII, 7.

40

game which we hunt is the fun of the chase: we are inexcusable if we pursue it badly or foolishly: it is quite another thing if we fail to make a kill. For we are born to go in quest of truth: to take possession of it is the property of a greater Power. Truth is not (as Democritus said) hidden in the bottom of an abyss: it is, rather, raised infinitely high within the knowledge of God.

This world is but a school of inquiry. The question is not who will spear the ring but who will make the best charges at it. The man who says what is true can act as foolishly as the one who says what is untrue: we are talking about the way you say it not what you say. My humour is to consider the form as much as the substance, and the barrister as much as his case, as Alcibiades told us to. Every day I spend time reading my authors, not caring about their learning, looking not for their subject-matter but how they handle it; just as I go in pursuit of discussions with a celebrated mind not to be taught by it but to get to know it.

Any man may speak truly: few men can speak ordinately, wisely, adequately. And so errors which proceed from ignorance do not offend me: absurdity does. I have often broken off discussing a bargain, even one advantageous to me, because of the silly claims of those I was bargaining with. For their mistakes I do not lose my temper above once a year with any of those who are subject to my authority, but when the point is the stupidity of their assertions or the obstinacy of their asinine excuses and their daft defences, then we are daily at each other's throats. They understand neither why nor what they are told: they answer accordingly. It is enough to make you despair. It is only when my head bangs against another head that I feel a big bump: I can come to terms with the failings of my servants better than with their thoughtlessness, insolence and downright silliness. Let them do less, provided that they can do something! You live in hope of making their wills warm to their work: but there is nothing to get from a block-head, nothing to hope for.

Yes, but what if I myself am taking things for other than they are? That may well be: that explains first of all why I condemn my inability to put up with it, holding it to be equally a defect in those who are right and those who are wrong, since there is always an element of tyrannical bad temper in being unable to tolerate charac-ters different from your own. Secondly, there is in truth no greater silliness, none more enduring, than to be provoked and enraged by the silliness of this world – and there is none more bizarre. For it makes you principally irritated with yourself: that philosopher of old would never have lacked occasion for his tears if he had concen-trated on himself.* One of the Seven Sages, Myson, was of the same humour as Timon and Democritus: when asked what he was laughing at all by himself, he replied, 'At the fact that I am laughing all by myself.'

How many statements and replies do I make every day which are silly by my norms – so even more fre-quently, to be sure, by the standards of others! If I bite my lips for them, what must the others be doing! To

---

* Heraclitus, the Sage who wept at the folly of the world; normally coupled with Democritus, who laughed at it. Followed by the most famous saying of Myson (Erasmus, *Apophthegmata*, VII, *Myson*, I).

sum up, we have to live among the living and let the stream flow under the bridge without worrying about it or, at very least, without making ourselves ill over it. Indeed, why can we encounter a man with a twisted deformed body without getting irritated, yet are unable to tolerate a deranged mind without flying into a rage?* Such harshness is vitiated and derives from the critic rather than the fault. Let us always have Plato's saying on our lips: 'If I find ill in something may it not be because I myself am ill? Am I not the one at fault? May my own criticism not be turned against me?' A wise and inspired refrain which chastises the most common and universal error of mankind. It is not merely the reproaches which we make to each other which can be regularly turned against us but also our reasons and our arguments in matters of controversy: we run ourselves through with our own swords. As it was ingeniously and aptly put by the man who first said it: '*Stercus cuique suum bene olet.*' [Everyone's shit smells good to himself.]†

Our eyes see nothing behind us. A hundred times a day when we go mocking our neighbour we are really mocking ourselves; we abominate in others those faults which are most manifestly our own, and, with a miraculous lack of shame and perspicacity, are astonished by them. Only yesterday I was able to watch an intelligent nobleman making jokes, as good as they were pertinent, about the silly way in which another nobleman went bashing everyone's ear about his family-tree and

* Plutarch (tr. Amyot), *Comment on pourra recevoir utilité de ses ennemis*, 110 E–F (and for Plato's saying about to be quoted).
† Erasmus, *Adages*, III, IV, II.

his family alliances, more than half of which were false, that kind of man being most inclined to launch out on such stupid subjects when his escutcheon is more dubious and least certain: yet he too, if he had stood back and looked at himself, would have discovered that he was hardly less extravagant in broadcasting and less boring in stressing the claims to precedence of his wife's family. What a dangerous arrogance with which a wife is seen to be armed at the hands of her very husband! If they understood Latin we ought to say to such people:

Age! si haec non insanit satis sua sponte, instiga!
[That's the way! If she is not mad enough herself, egg her on!]*

I do not mean that nobody should make indictments unless he is spotless; if that were so no one would make them. What I mean is that when our judgement brings a charge against another man over a matter then in question, it must not exempt us from an internal judicial inquiry. It is a work of charity for a man who is unable to weed out a defect in himself to try, nevertheless, to weed it out in another in whom the seedling may be less malignant and stubborn. And it never seems to me to be an appropriate answer to anyone who warns me of a fault in me to say that he has it too. What difference does that make? The warning remains true and useful. If we had sound nostrils our shit ought to stink all the more for its being our own. Socrates was convinced that

* Terence, *Andria*, IV, ii, 9.

if there was a man who, together with his son and a stranger, was found guilty of violence or injury, that man should begin with himself, first presenting himself to be sentenced by the judge and to beg for expiation at the hands of the executioner; next, he should present his son; then the stranger.* If that precept pitches it rather too high, at least he should be the first to be presented before his own conscience for punishment.

Our first judges are properly our senses, which perceive things only by their external accidents. No wonder then that in all the elements which contribute to our society there is such a constant and universal addition of surface appearances and ritual; with the result that the best and most effective part of our polities consists in that. We are always dealing with Man, whose nature is wondrously corporeal. Those who in recent years have wished to build up for us so contemplative and non-material an exercise of worship should not be astonished if there are those who think that it would have slipped and melted through their fingers if it did not keep a hold among us as a mark, sign and means of division and of faction rather than for itself.

It is the same in discussion: the gravity, academic robes and rank of the man who is speaking often lend credence to arguments which are vain and silly. Who could believe that so redoubtable a lord with so great a retinue does not have within him some more-than-ordinary talent, or that a man who is entrusted with so many missions and offices of state, a man so disdainful

* Plato, *Gorgias*, 480 B–C.

and so arrogant, is not cleverer than another man who bows to him from afar and whom nobody ever employs! Not only the words of such people but their very grimaces are watched and put to their account, each man striving to give them some fine solid significance. If they condescend to join in ordinary discussions and you show them anything but approval and reverence, they clobber you with the authority of their experience: they have heard this; they have seen that; they have done this: you are overwhelmed with cases. I would like to tell such men that the fruit of a surgeon's experience lies not in a recital of his operations nor in his reminding us that he has cured four patients of the plague and three of the gout, unless he knows how to extract from them material for forming his judgement and unless he knows how to convince us that he has been made wiser by the practice of his medical art. So, in a consort of instruments, we do not hear the lute, the spinet and the flute but a global harmony, the fruit resulting from the combination of the entire group.

If they have been improved by their missions and their travels that should appear in the products of their understanding. It is not enough to relate our experiences: we must weigh them and group them; we must also have digested them and distilled them so as to draw out the reasons and conclusions they comport. There never were so many writing history! It is always good and profitable to listen to them, for they furnish us with ample instruction, fine and praiseworthy, from the store-house of their memory: that is certainly of great value in helping us to live. But we are not looking for that at the moment: we are trying to find out whether the chroniclers and compilers are themselves worthy of praise.

I loathe all tyranny, both in speech and action. I like to brace myself against those trivial incidentals which cheat our judgement via our senses; and by keeping a watchful eye on men of extraordinary rank I have discovered that they are, for the most part, just like the rest of us:

> *Rarus enim ferme sensus communis in illa*
> *Fortuna.*
>
> [Common sense is rare enough in that high station.]*

Perhaps we esteem them and perceive them for less than they are, because they undertake to do more and so reveal themselves more. The porter must be stronger and tougher than his load. The man who has not had to use all his strength leaves you to guess whether he has any more in reserve, whether he has been assayed to the ultimate point: the man who succumbs under the weight betrays his limitations and the weakness of his shoulders. That is why, more than other people, so many of the learned can be seen to have inadequate souls. They could have been good farmers, good merchants, good craftsmen: their natural forces were tailored to such proportions. Knowledge is a very weighty thing: they sink beneath it. Their mental apparatus has not enough energy nor skill to display that noble material and to

* Juvenal, *Satires*, VIII, 73–4.

apportion its strength, to exploit it and to make it help them. Knowledge can lodge only in a powerful nature: and that is very rare. Feeble minds, said Socrates, corrupt the dignity of philosophy when they handle it; she appears to be useless and defective when sheathed in a bad covering.*

That is how they grow rotten and besotted,

> *Humani qualis simulator simius oris,*
> *Quem puer arridens pretioso stamine serum*
> *Velavit, nudasque nates ac terga reliquit,*
> *Ludibrium mensis.*

[Like an ape, that imitator of the human face, which a boy dresses up, for a laugh, in precious silken robes, leaving the cheeks of its backside bare to amuse the guests at table.]

It is the same for those who rule over us and give orders, who hold the world in their hands: it is not enough for them to have an ordinary intelligence, to be able to achieve what we can. They are far beneath us if they are not way above us. Since they promise more, they owe more too; that is why keeping silent is not, in their case, merely a courteous and grave demeanour; it is also more often a profitable and gainful one. For when Megabysus went to see Appelles in his studio, he long remained silent. But when he began to discourse on the works of art, he received this rude reprimand: 'While you kept silent you appeared to be a great Somebody because of your chains-of-office and your retinue, but

* Perhaps a reference to Plato, *Republic*, VI, 495 C–D.

48

now we have heard you talk the very apprentices in my workshop despise you.'* Those magnificent decorations, that grand estate would not tolerate ordinary plebeian ignorance in him, nor inappropriate comments on paintings: he should have maintained that outward presumed connoisseurship. For how many men in my time has a cold, taciturn mien served their silly souls as signs of wisdom and ability!

Of necessity dignities and offices are bestowed more by fortune than by merit: you often do wrong to blame kings for that. On the contrary, it is a wonder that they have such good luck, enjoying as they do so few ways of finding out.

Principis est virtus maxima nosse suos,
[For a prince, the chief merit is to know his subjects,]†

for Nature has not given them eyes which can extend over so many peoples, distinguishing pre-eminence and seeing into our bosoms, where is lodged the knowledge of our will and of our better qualities. They have to select us by fumbling guesses: by our family, our wealth, our learning and the voice of the people – the feeblest of arguments. Anyone who could discover the means by which men could be justly judged and reasonably chosen would, at a stroke, establish a perfect form of commonwealth.

'Yes. But he brought this great matter to a successful conclusion.' – That means something, but not enough;

* Erasmus, *Apophthegmata*, VI, *Diversorum Graecorum*, XXXII.
† Martial, *Epigrams*, VIII, 15.

for we rightly accept the maxim which says that plans must not be judged by results. The Carthaginians punished bad counsels in their captains even when they were put right by a happy outcome. And the Roman people often refused to mark great and beneficial victories because the qualities of leadership of the commander were inferior to his good luck. In this world's activities we often notice that Fortune rivals Virtue: she shows us what power she has over everything and delights in striking down our presumption by making the incompetent lucky since she cannot make them wise. She loves to interfere, favouring those performances whose course has been entirely her own. That is why we can see, every day, the simplest among us bringing the greatest public and private tasks to successful conclusions.

Siramnes the Persian replied to those who were amazed that his enterprises turned out so badly, seeing that his projects were so wise, by saying that he alone was master of his projects while Fortune was mistress of the outcome of his enterprises: they too could make the same reply to explain the opposite tendency.*

Most of this world's events happen by themselves:

> *Fata viam inveniunt.*
> [The Fates find a way.]†

The outcome often lends authority to the most inept leadership. Our intervention is virtually no more than a

---

* Cited by Amyot in his Prologue to *Les Vies de Plutarque*.
† Virgil, *Aeneid*, III, 395; then, Horace, *Odes*, I, ix, 9.

habit, the result of tradition and example rather than of reason. I was once astounded by the greatness of a venture; I then learnt from those who had brought it to a successful conclusion what their motives were and what methods they used: I found nothing but ordinary notions.

Indeed the most ordinary usual ones are also perhaps the most reliable and the most suitable in practice if not for show. What if the most lowly reasons are the most solidly based? What if the most humble, most lax and best-trodden ones are the most suited to our concerns? If we are to safeguard the authority of the Privy Council we do not need laymen participating in it nor seeing further than the first obstacle. If we want to maintain its reputation it must be taken on trust, as a whole.

My thought sketches out the matter for a while and dwells lightly on the first aspects of it: then I usually leave the principal thrust of the task to heaven.

> *Permitte divis caetera.*
> [Entrust the rest to the gods.]

To my mind Good Luck and Bad Luck are two sovereign powers. There is no wisdom in thinking that the role of Fortune can be played by human wisdom. What he undertakes is vain if a man should presume to embrace both causes and consequences and to lead the progress of his action by the hand; and it is especially vain in counsels of war. Never were there more military circum-spection and prudence than I sometimes see practised among us: perhaps we fear that we shall get lost en route, and therefore keep ourselves in reserve for the climax in the final act!

I will go on to say that our very wisdom and mature reflections are for the most part led by chance. My will and my reasoning are stirred this way and that. And many of their movements govern themselves without me. My reason is daily subject to incitements and agitations which are due to chance:

> *Vertuntur species animorum, et pectora motus*
> *Nunc alios, alios dum nubila ventus agebat,*
> *Concipiunt.*

[Their minds' ideas are ever turning round; the emotions in their breasts are driven hither and thither like clouds before the wind.]*

Look and see who wield most power in our cities; who do their jobs best. You will find that they are usually the least clever. There have been cases when women, children and lunatics have ruled their states equally as well as the most talented princes. Coarse men more usually succeed in such things, says Thucydides, better than the subtle ones do.† We ascribe the deeds of their good fortune to their wisdom.

> *Ut quisque fortuna utitur*
> *Ita praecellet, atque exinde sapere illum omnes dicimus.*

---

* Virgil, *Georgics*, I, 420–2.
† Thucydides, cited (with others of the above) from Justus Lipsius' *Politici*, as is the following, from Plautus' *Pseudolus*.

[Each outstanding man is raised by his good fortune; we then say that he is clever.]

That is why I insist that, in all our activities, their outcomes provide meagre testimony of our worth and ability.

Now I was just about to say that it merely suffices for us to see a man raised to great dignity; even though we knew him three days before to be a negligible man, there seeps into our opinions, unawares, a notion of greatness, of talents, and we convince ourselves that by growing in style and reputation he has grown in merit. Our judgements of him are not based on his worth but (as is the case with the counters of an abacus) on the tokens of rank. Let his luck turn again, let him have a fall and be lost in the crowd again, then we all ask in wonder what had made him soar so high! 'Is this the same man?' we ask. 'Did he not know more about it when he was up there? Are princes satisfied with so little? We were in good hands, indeed we were!'

That is something I have seen many times in my own days.

Why, even the mask of greatness which is staged in our plays affects us somewhat and deceives us. What I worship in kings is the crowd of their worshippers. Everything should bow and submit to our kings – except our intelligence. My reason was not made for bending and bowing, my knees were.

When Melanthius was asked how Dionysius' tragedy appeared to him, 'I never saw it,' he replied. 'It was obscured by the words!' So, too, most of those who judge what the great have to say ought to answer: 'I never heard his words: they were too much obscured by his dignity, grandeur and majesty.'*

One day, when Antisthenes urged the Athenians to command that donkeys be used, as their horses were, to plough their fields, he was told that donkeys were not born for such a service. 'That does not matter,' he retorted. 'It all depends on your issuing the order: for the most ignorant and incompetent men whom you put in command of your wars never fail to become suddenly most worthy of command, because it is you who employ them!'†

Related to this is the practice of so many people to sanctify the kings whom they have chosen from among themselves. They are not contented with honouring them: they need to worship them. The people of Mexico dare not look at the face of their king once they have completed the rites of his enthronement, but as though they had deified him by his royal state they make him swear not merely to maintain their religion, laws and liberties and to be valiant, just and debonair, he must also swear to cause the sun to run shining with its accustomed light, the clouds to break in due season, the rivers to flow in their courses and the earth to bring forth all things needful for his people.‡

I am opposed to that widespread fashion and I most doubt a man's ability when I see it accompanied by great rank and public acclaim. We should remember what it

* Plutarch (tr. Amyot), *Comment il faut ouïr*, 64 H.
† Erasmus, *Apophthegmata*, VII, *Antisthenes*, XXX.
‡ Lopez de Gomara (tr. Fumée), *Histoire générale des Indes*, II, lxxvii.

means to a man to be able to speak when he wants to, to choose the right moment, to break off the discussion or switch the subject with the authority of a master, to defend himself against objections with a shake of the head, a little smile or with silence, in front of courtiers who tremble with reverence and respect.

A monstrously rich man, when some trivial matter was being aired casually over dinner, joined in the discussion and began with these very words: 'Anyone who says otherwise is either ignorant or a liar,' and so on. You had better follow up that philosophical thrust with a dagger in your hand!

Here is another warning, which I find most useful: in debates and discussions we should not immediately be impressed by what we take to be a man's own *bons mots*. Most men are rich with other men's abilities. It may well be that such-and-such a man makes a fine remark, a good reply or a pithy saying, advancing it without realizing its power. (That we do not grasp everything we borrow can doubtless be proved from my own case.) We should not always give way, no matter what beauty or truth it may have. We should either seriously attack it or else, under pretence of not understanding it, retreat a little so as to probe it thoroughly and to discover how it is lodged in its author. We may be helping his sword-thrust to carry beyond his reach, running on to it ourselves. There have been times when, pressed by necessity in the duel of words, I have made counter-attacks which struck home more than I ever hoped or expected. I was counting their number: they were accepted for their weight.

When I am disputing with a man of strong arguments

I enjoy anticipating his conclusions; I save him the bother of explaining himself; I make an assay at forestalling his ideas while they are still unfinished and being formed (the order and stretch of his intelligence warn me and threaten me from afar). Similarly, with those others I mentioned I do quite the opposite: we should suppose nothing, understand nothing but what they explain. If their judgements are apposite but expressed in universals – 'This is good: that is bad' – find out whether it is luck which makes them apposite. Make them circumscribe and restrict their verdict a little: 'Why is it good? How is it good?' Those universal judgements (which I find so common) say nothing. They are like those who greet people as a mass or a crowd: those who have genuine knowledge of them greet them by name and distinguish them as individuals. But it is a chancy business. Which explains why, on average more than once a day, I have seen men with ill-founded minds trying to act clever by showing me some beautiful detail in the book they are reading, but choosing so badly the point on which they fix their admiration that instead of revealing the excellence of their author they reveal their own ignorance.

When you have just listened to a whole page of Virgil you can safely exclaim, 'Now that is beautiful!' The cunning ones escape that way. But to undertake to go back over the detail of a good author, to try to indicate with precise and selected examples where he surpasses himself and where he flies high by weighing his words and his locutions and his choice of materials one after another: not many try that. '*Videndum est non modo quid quisque loquatur, sed etiam quid quisque sentiat, atque etiam* *qua de causa quisque sentiat.'* [We should not only examine what each one says, but what are his opinions and what grounds he has for holding them.]* Day after day I hear stupid people uttering words which are not stupid. They say something good; let us discover how deeply they understand it and where they got hold of it. They do not own that fine saying or that fine reasoning, but we help them to use it. They are only looking after it. Perhaps they only produced it fortuitously, hesitantly: it is we who give it credit and value. You are lending them a hand. But why? They feel no gratitude towards you for it and become all the more silly. Do not support them; let them go their own way: they will handle that material like a man who fears getting scalded: they dare not show it in a different light or context nor to deepen it. Give it the tiniest shaking and it slips away from them: then, strong and beautiful though it be, they surrender it to you. They have beautiful weapons, but the handles are loose! How often have I learnt that from experience!

Now, if you come and clarify and reinforce it for them, they immediately take advantage of your interpretation and rob you of it: 'That is what I was about to say,' or, 'That is how I understand it, exactly,' or, 'If I did not put it that way it was because I could not find the right words.' – Bluster on! We should use even cunning to punish such arrogant stupidity.

Hegesias' principle that we should neither hate nor blame but instruct is right elsewhere but not here.†

* Cicero, *De officiis*, I, xli, 147.
† Diogenes Laertius, *Life of Aristippus*.

There is neither justice nor kindness in helping a man to get up who does not know how to use your help and who is all the worse for it. I like to let them sink deeper in the mire and to get even more entangled – so deeply that, if possible, even they finally realize it!

You cannot cure silliness and unreasonableness by one act of warning. Of that sort of cure we can properly say what Cyrus replied to the man who urged him to give an exhortation to his troops at the moment of battle: that men are not made courageous warriors on the battlefield by a good harangue any more than you can become a good musician by hearing a good song.* Apprenticeships must be served, before you set hand to anything, by long and sustained study.

It is to our own folk that we owe this obligation to be assiduous in correcting and instructing; but to go preaching at the first passer-by or to read lectures on ignorance and silliness to the first man we come across is a practice which I loathe. I rarely do it during dis-cussions in which I am involved; I prefer to let it all go by rather than to resort to such remote and donnish lecturing. My humour is unsuited, both in speaking and writing, to those who are learning first principles. But however false or absurd I judge things to be which are said in company or before a third party, I never leap in to interrupt them by word or gesture.

Meanwhile nothing in stupidity irritates me more than its being much more pleased with itself than any reasonableness could reasonably be. It is a disaster that

---

* Xenophon, *Cyropaedia*, III, iii, 49–50.

wisdom forbids you to be satisfied with yourself and always sends you away dissatisfied and fearful, whereas stubbornness and foolhardiness fill their hosts with joy and assurance. It is the least clever of men who look down at others over their shoulders, always returning from the fray full of glory and joyfulness. And as often as not their haughty language and their happy faces win them victory in the eyes of the bystanders who are generally feeble in judging and incapable of discerning real superiority. The surest proof of animal-stupidity is ardent obstinacy of opinion. Is there anything more certain, decided, disdainful, contemplative, grave and serious, than a donkey?

Perhaps we may include in the category of conversation and discussion those short pointed exchanges which happiness and intimacy introduce among friends when pleasantly joking together and sharply mocking each other. That is a sport for which my natural gaiety makes me rather well-suited; and if it is not as tensely serious as the other sport I have just described, it is no less keen and clever, nor, as it seemed to Lycurgus, any less useful. Where I am concerned I contribute more licence than wit, being more happy in that than in finding my material; but I am a perfect target, for I can put up with retaliation without getting angry not merely when sharp but even when rude. When I am suddenly attacked, if I cannot at once find a good repartee I do not waste time following up that thrust with vague boring contestations akin to stubbornness but I let it go by, cheerfully flapping down my ears and waiting for a better moment to get my own back. No huckster wins every haggle.

Most people, when their arguments fail, change voice and expression, and instead of retrieving themselves betray their weaknesses and susceptibility by an unmannerly anger. In the excitement of jesting we can sometimes nip those secret chords of one another's imperfections which we cannot even pluck without offence when we are calm; we warn each other profitably of each other's faults. There are other sports, physical ones, rash and harsh in the French manner, which I hate unto death. I am touchy and sensitive about such things: in my lifetime I have seen two princes of the blood royal laid in their graves because of them. It is an ugly thing to fight for fun.*

In addition when I want to judge another man I ask him to what extent he is himself satisfied; how far he is happy with what he has said or written. I want him to avoid those fine excuses: 'I was only playing at it' –

> *Ablatum mediis opus est incudibus istud*
> [It was taken off the anvil only half finished]†

– 'I only spent an hour on it'; 'I have not seen it since'. – 'All right,' I say: 'let us leave those examples. Show me something which does represent you entirely, something by which you are happy to be measured.' And then I say, 'What do you consider the most beautiful aspect of your work? Is it this quality or that quality? Is it its

---

* Henry II was killed while jousting; Henry, Marquess of Beaupréau died of wounds received in a tournament.
† Ovid, *Tristia*, I, vii, 9.

gracious style, its subject-matter, your discovery of the material, your judgement, your erudition?'

For I normally find that men are as wrong in judging their own work as other people's, not simply because their emotions are involved but because they lack the ability to understand it and to analyse it. The work itself, by its own momentum and fortune, can favour the author beyond his own understanding and research; it can run ahead of him. There is no work that I can judge with less certainty than my own: the *Essays* I place – very hesitantly and with little assurance – sometimes low, sometimes high.

Many books are useful for their subject-matter: their authors derive little glory from them. And there are good books which as far as good workmanship is concerned are a disgrace to their authors. I could write about our style of feasting, about our clothing – and I could write it gracelessly; I could publish contemporary edicts and the letters of princes which come into the public domain; I could make an abridgement of a good book (and every abridgement of a good book is a daft one) and then the book itself could chance to get lost. Things like that. From such compilations posterity would derive unique assistance: but what honour would I derive from them except for being lucky? A good proportion of famous books fall in that category.

When I was reading a few years ago Philippe de Commines – a very good author, certainly – I noted the following saying as being above average: 'We should be wary of doing such great services to our master that we render him unable to reward them justly.' I should have praised not him but his discovery of a topic. Not long ago I came upon this sentence in Tacitus: *'Beneficia eo usque laeta sunt dum videntur exolvi posse; ubi multum antevenere, pro gratia odium redditur.'* [Good turns are pleasing only in so far as they seem repayable. Much beyond that we repay with hatred not gratitude.] Seneca puts it forcefully: *'Nam qui putat esse turpe non reddere, non vult esse cui reddat.'* [He for whom not to repay is a disgrace wants his benefactor dead.] Quintus Cicero, with a laxer turn of phrase, writes: *'Qui se non putat satisfacere, amicus esse nullo modo potest.'* [He who cannot repay his debt to you can in no wise love you.]*

An author's subject can, when appropriate, show him to be erudite or retentive, but if you are to judge what qualities in him most truly belong to him and are the most honourable (I mean the force and beauty of his soul) you must know what is really his and what definitely is not; and in that which is not, how much we are indebted to him for his selection, disposition, ornamentation and the literary quality of what he had contributed. Supposing he has taken somebody else's matter and then ruined the style, as often happens! People like us who have little experience of books are in difficulties when we come across some fine example of ingenuity in a modern poet or some strong argument in a preacher. We dare not praise them for it before we have learned from a scholar whether that item is original to them or taken from another. Until I have done that I remain suspicious.

* Philippe de Commines, III, xii; Tacitus, *Annals*, IV, xviii; Seneca, *Epist. moral.*, LXXXVI, 32; Cicero, *De petitione consultatus*, ix.

I have just read through at one go Tacitus' *History*
(something which rarely happens to me: it is twenty
years since I spent one full hour at a time on a book. I
did it on the recommendation of a nobleman highly
esteemed in France both for his own virtue and for that
sustained quality of ability and goodness which he is
seen to share with his many brothers). I know of no
author who combines a chronicle of public events with
so much reflection on individual morals and biases. And
it appears to me (contrary to what appears to him) that,
as he has the particular task of following the careers of
the contemporary Emperors (men so odd and so extreme
in their various characters) as well as the noteworthy
deeds which they provoked in their subjects above all by
their cruelty, he has a more striking and interesting topic
to relate and discourse upon than if he had to tell of
battles and world revolutions. Consequently I find him
unprofitable when he dashes through those fair, noble
deaths as though he were afraid of tiring us by accounts
both too long and too numerous.

This manner of history is by far the most useful. The
unrolling of public events depends more on the guiding
hand of Fortune: that of private ones, on our own.
Tacitus' work is more a judgement on historical events
than a narration of them. There are more precepts than
accounts. It is not a book to be read but one to be studied
and learnt. It is so full of aphorisms that, apposite or not,
they are everywhere. It is a seed-bed of ethical and
political arguments to supply and adorn those who hold
high rank in the governing of this world. He pleads his
case with solid and vigorous reasons, in an epigrammatic

and exquisite style following the affected manner of his century. (They were so fond of a high style that when they found no wit or subtlety in their subject-matter they resorted to witty subtle words.) He is not all that different from Seneca, but while he seems to have more flesh on him Seneca is more acute. Tacitus can more properly serve a sickly troubled nation like our own is at present: you could often believe that we were the subject of his narrating and berating. Those who doubt his good faith clearly betray that they resent him from prejudice. He has sound opinions and inclines to the right side in the affairs of Rome. I do regret though that, by making Pompey no better than Marius and Scylla only more secretive, he judged him more harshly than is suggested by the verdict of men who lived and dealt with him.* True, Pompey's striving to govern affairs has not been cleared of ambition nor a wish for vengeance: even his friends feared that victory might make him go out of his mind, though not to the extremes of insanity of those other two. Nothing in his life suggests to us the menace of such express tyranny and cruelty. Besides we ought never to let suspicions outweigh evidence: so on this point I do not trust Tacitus.

That the accounts which he gives are indeed simple and straight can perhaps be argued from the very fact that they do not exactly fit his concluding judgements, to which he is led by the slant he had adopted; they often go beyond the evidence which he provides – which he had not deigned to bias in the slightest degree. He needs

* Tacitus, *Histories*, II, xxxviii.

no defence for having assented to the religion of his day, in accordance with the laws which bade him to do so, and for being ignorant of the true religion. That is his misfortune not his fault.

What I have chiefly been considering is his judgement: I am not entirely clear about it. For example, take these words from the letter sent to the Senate by the aged ailing Tiberius: 'What, Sirs, should I write to you, what indeed should I not write to you at this time? I know that I am daily nearing death; may the gods and goddesses make my end worse if I know what to write.' I cannot see why he applies them with such certainty to a poignant remorse tormenting Tiberius' conscience. Leastways when I came across them I saw no such thing.*

It also seemed to me a bit weak of him when he was obliged to mention that he had once held an honourable magistracy in Rome to go on and explain that he was not referring to it in order to boast about it. That line seemed rather shoddy to me for a soul such as his: not to dare to talk roundly of yourself betrays a defect of thought. A man of straight and elevated mind who judges surely and soundly employs in all circumstances examples taken from himself as well as from others, and frankly cites himself as witness as well as third parties. We should jump over those plebeian rules of etiquette in favour of truth and freedom. I not only dare to talk about myself but to talk of nothing but myself. I am wandering off the point when I write of anything else, cheating my subject of *me*. I do not love myself with

* Tacitus, *Annals*, VI, vi.

such lack of discretion, nor am I so bound and involved in myself, that I am unable to see myself apart and to consider myself separately as I would a neighbour or a tree. The error is the same if you fail to see the limits of your worth or if you report more than you can see. We owe more love to God than to ourselves. We know him less, yet talk about him till we are glutted.

If Tacitus' writings tell us anything at all about his character, he was a very great man, upright and courageous, whose virtue was not of the superstitious kind but philosophical and magnanimous. You could find some of his testimony rather rash; for example he maintains that when a soldier's hands grew stiff with the cold while carrying a pile of wood they adhered to his load, broke away from his arms and stuck there dead.* In similar cases my custom is to bow to the authority of such great witnesses. When he says that, by favour of Serapis the god, Vespasian cured a blind woman in Alexandria by anointing her eyes with his saliva and also performed some additional miracle or other, he was following the dutiful example of all good historians who keep a chronicle of important happenings: included among public events are popular rumours and opinions. Their role is to give an account of popular beliefs, not to account for them: which part is played by Theologians and philosophers as directors of consciences. That is why his fellow-historian, great man as he was, most wisely said: '*Equidem plura transcribo quam credo: nam nec*

---

* Tacitus, *Annals*, XIII, xxxv; then, IV, lxxi (seen by some as a parody of Christ's curing the blind man in Mark 8:23).

affirmare sustineo, de quibus dubito, nec subducere quae accepi.' [I do indeed pass on more than I believe. I cannot vouch for the things which I doubt, nor can I omit what I have been told by tradition.] And another says: *'Haec neque affirmare, neque refellere operae pretium est: famae rerum standum est.'* [These things are neither to be vouched for nor denied: we must cling to tradition.]*

Tacitus, writing during a period in which belief in portents was on the wane, says that he nevertheless does not wish to fail to provide a foothold for them, and so includes in his *Annals* matters accepted by so many decent people with so great a reverence for antiquity.

That is very well said. Let them pass on their histories to us according to what they find received, not according to their own estimate. I, who am monarch of the subject which I treat and not accountable for it to anyone, do not for all that believe everything I say. Sometimes my mind launches out with paradoxes which I mistrust and with verbal subtleties which make me shake my head; but I let them take their chance. I know that some men gain a reputation from such things. It is not for me alone to judge them. I describe myself standing up and lying down, from front and back, from right and left and with all my inborn complexities. Even minds of sustained power are not always sustained in their application and discernment.

That is, *grosso modo*, the Tacitus which is presented to me, vaguely enough, by my memory. All *grosso-modo* judgements are lax and defective.

---

* Quintus Curtius, IX, i; Livy, VIII, vi.

4
On idleness

Just as fallow lands, when rich and fertile, are seen to abound in hundreds and thousands of different kinds of useless weeds so that, if we would make them do their duty, we must subdue them and keep them busy with seeds specifically sown for our service; and just as women left alone may sometimes be seen to produce shapeless lumps of flesh but need to be kept busy by a semen other than her own in order to produce good natural offspring: so too with our minds. If we do not keep them busy with some particular subject which can serve as a bridle to reign them in, they charge ungovernably about, ranging to and fro over the wastelands of our thoughts:

> *Sicut aquae tremulum labris ubi lumen ahenis*
> *Sole repercussum, aut radiantis imagine Lunae*
> *Omnia pervolitat late loca jamque sub auras*
> *Erigitur, summique ferit laquearia tecti.*

[As when ruffled water in a bronze pot reflects the light of the sun and the shining face of the moon, sending shimmers flying high into the air and striking against the panelled ceilings].*

* Virgil, *Aeneid*, VIII, 22.

Then, there is no madness, no raving lunacy, which such agitations do not bring forth:

> *velut aegri somnia, vanae*
> *Finguntur species.*

[they fashion vain apparitions as in the dreams of sick men.]*

When the soul is without a definite aim she gets lost; for, as they say, if you are everywhere you are nowhere.

> *Quisquis ubique habitat, Maxime, nusquam habitat.*

[Whoever dwells everywhere, Maximus, dwells nowhere at all.]†

Recently I retired to my estates, determined to devote myself as far as I could to spending what little life I have left quietly and privately; it seemed to me then that the greatest favour I could do for my mind was to leave it in total idleness, caring for itself, concerned only with itself, calmly thinking of itself. I hoped it could do that more easily from then on, since with the passage of time it had grown mature and put on weight.

But I find –

> *Variam semper dant otia mentis*

[Idleness always produces fickle changes of mind].‡

– that on the contrary it bolted off like a runaway horse, taking far more trouble over itself than it ever did over

---

* Horace, *Ars poetica*, 7.   † Martial, VII, lxxiii.
‡ Lucan, *Pharsalia*, IV, 704.

anyone else; it gives birth to so many chimeras and fantastic monstrosities, one after another, without order or fitness, that, so as to contemplate at my ease their oddness and their strangeness, I began to keep a record of them, hoping in time to make my mind ashamed of itself.

5

On the affection of fathers for their children

For Madame d'Estissac

Madame: unless I am saved by oddness or novelty (qualities which usually give value to anything) I shall never extricate myself with honour from this daft undertaking; but it is so fantastical and presents an aspect so totally unlike normal practice that it may just get by.

It was a melancholy humour (and therefore a humour most inimical to my natural complexion) brought on by the chagrin caused by the solitary retreat I plunged myself into a few years ago, which first put into my head this raving concern with writing. Finding myself quite empty, with nothing to write about, I offered myself to myself as theme and subject matter. It is the only book of its kind in the world, in its conception wild and fantastically eccentric. Nothing in this work of mine is worthy of notice except that bizarre quality, for the best craftsman in the world would not know how to fashion anything remarkable out of material so vacuous and base.

Now, Madame, having decided to draw a portrait of myself from life, I would have overlooked an important feature if I had failed to portray the honour which I have always shown you for your great merits. I particularly wanted to do so at the head of this chapter, since of all your fine qualities one of the first in rank is the love you show your children.

Anyone who knows how young you were when your husband Monsieur d'Estissac left you a widow; the proposals which have been made to you by such great and honourable men (as many as to any lady of your condition in France); the constancy and firmness of purpose with which you have, for so many years and through so many difficulties, carried the weight of responsibility for your children's affairs (which have kept you busy in so many corners of France and still besiege you); and the happy prosperity which your wisdom or good fortune have brought to those affairs: he will readily agree with me that we have not one single example of maternal love today more striking than your own.

I praise God, Madame, that your love has been so well employed. For the great hopes of himself raised by your boy, Monsieur d'Estissac, amply assure us that when he comes of age you will be rewarded by the duty and gratitude of an excellent son. But he is still a child, unable to appreciate the innumerable acts of devotion he has received from you: so I should like him, if this book should fall into his hands one day, to be able to learn something from me at a time when I shall not even have a mouth to tell it to him – something I can vouch for quite truthfully and which will be made even more vigorously evident, God willing, by the good effects he will be aware of in himself: namely, that there is no nobleman in France who owes more to his mother than he does, and that in the future he will be able to give no more certain proof of his goodness and virtue than by acknowledging your qualities.

If there truly is a Law of Nature – that is to say, an instinct which can be seen to be universally and permanently stamped on the beasts and on ourselves (which is not beyond dispute) – I would say that, in my opinion, following hard on the concern for self-preservation and the avoidance of whatever is harmful, there would come second the love which the begetter feels for the begotten. And since Nature seems to have committed this love to us out of a concern for the effective propagation of the successive parts of the world which she has contrived, it is not surprising if love is not so great when we go backwards, from children to fathers. To which we may add a consideration taken from Aristotle,* that anyone who does a kindness to another loves him more than he is loved in return; that anyone to whom a debt is owed feels greater love than the one by whom the debt is owed; and that every creator loves what he has made more than it would love him if it were capable of emotions. This is especially true because each holds his *being* dear: and *being* consists in motion and activity; in a sense, therefore, everyone is, to some degree, within anything he does: the benefactor has performed an action both fair and noble: the recipient, on the other hand, has only performed a useful one, and mere usefulness is less lovable than nobility. Nobility is stable and lasting, furnishing the one who has practised

---

* Aristotle, *Nicomachaean Ethics*, IX, vii, 4–6.

it with a constant satisfaction. Usefulness, however, can easily disappear or diminish, and the memory of it is neither so refreshing nor so sweet. The things which have cost us most are dearest to us – and it costs us more to give than to receive.

Since it has pleased God to bestow some slight capacity for discursive reasoning on us so that we should not be slavishly subject to the laws of Nature as the beasts are but should conform to them by our free-will and judgement, we should indeed make some concessions to the simple authority of the common laws of Nature but not allow ourselves to be swept tyrannously away by her: Reason alone must govern our inclinations.

For my part, those propensities which are produced in us without the command and mediation of our judgement taste strangely flat. In the case of the subject under discussion, I am incapable of finding a place for that emotion which leads people to cuddle new-born infants while they are still without movements of soul or recognizable features of body to make themselves lovable. And I have never willingly allowed them to be nursed in my presence. A true and well-regulated affection should be born, and then increase, as children enable us to get to know them; if they show they deserve it, we should cherish them with a truly fatherly love, since our natural propensity is then progressing side by side with reason; if they turn out differently, the same applies, *mutatis mutandis*: we should, despite the force of Nature, always yield to reason.

In fact, the very reverse often applies; we feel ourselves more moved by the skippings and jumpings and babyish tricks of our children than by their activities when they are fully formed, as though we had loved them not as human beings but only as playthings or as pet monkeys. Some fathers will give them plenty of toys when they are children but will resent the slightest expenditure on their needs once they have come of age. It even looks, in fact, as if we are jealous of seeing them cut a figure in the world, able to enjoy it just when we are on the point of leaving it, and that this makes us miserly and close-fisted towards them: it irritates us that they should come treading on our heels, as if to summon us to take our leave. Since in sober truth things are so ordered that children can only have their being and live their lives at the expense of our being and of our lives, we ought not to undertake to be fathers if that frightens us.

For my part, I find it cruel and unjust not to welcome them to a share and fellow-interest in our property – giving them full knowledge of our domestic affairs as co-partners when they are capable of it – and not to cut back on our own interests, economizing on them so as to provide for theirs, since we gave them birth for just such a purpose. It is unjust to see an aged father, broken and only half alive, stuck in his chimney-corner with the absolute possession of enough wealth to help and maintain several children, allowing them all this time to waste their best years without means of advancement in the public service and of making themselves better known. They are driven by despair to find some way, however unjust, of providing for their needs: I have seen in my time several young men of good family so addicted to larceny that no punishment could turn them from it.

I know one young man, very well connected, with whom I had a word about just such a matter at the earnest request of his brother, a brave and most honourable nobleman. In reply the young man admitted quite openly that he had been brought to such vile conduct by the unbending meanness of his father, adding that he had now grown so used to it that he could not stop himself. He had just been caught stealing rings from a lady whose morning reception he was attending with several others. It reminded me of a story I had heard about another nobleman who had so adapted himself to the exigencies of that fine profession that when he did become master of his inheritance and decided to give up this practice he nevertheless could not stop himself from stealing anything he needed when he passed by a stall, despite the bother of having to send somebody to pay for it later. I have known several people so trained and adapted to thieving that they regularly steal from their close companions things which they intend to return.

I may be a Gascon but there is no vice I can understand less. My complexion makes me loathe it rather more than my reason condemns it: I have never even wanted to steal anything from anyone. It is true that my part of the world is rather more infamous for theft than the rest of our French nation: yet we have all seen in our time, on several occasions, men of good family from other provinces convicted of many dreadful robberies. I am afraid that we must partly attribute such depravity to the fault of their fathers.

If anyone then tells me, as a very intelligent nobleman once did, that the only practical advantage he wanted to get from saving up all his money was to be honoured and courted by his children (since now that age had deprived him of strength that was the only remedy he had left against being treated with neglect and contempt by everybody, and so maintaining his authority over his family – and truly, not only old age but all forms of weakness are, according to Aristotle, great encouragements to miserliness)* – then there is something in that. But it is medicine to cure an illness the birth of which ought to have been prevented. A father is wretched indeed if he can only hold the love of his children – if you can call it love – by making them depend on his help.

We should make ourselves respected for our virtues and our abilities and loved for our goodness and gentlemanliness. The very ashes of a rare timber have their value, and we are accustomed to hold in respect and reverence the very bones and remains of honourable people. In the case of someone who has lived his life honourably, no old age can be so decrepit and smelly that it ceases to be venerable – especially to the children, whose souls should have been instructed in their duty not by need and want, nor by harshness nor force, but by reason:

> *et errat longe, mea quidem sententia,*
> *Qui imperium credat esse gravius aut stabilius*
> *Vi quod fit, quam illud quod amicitia adjungitur.*

---

* Aristotle, *Nicomachaean Ethics*, IV, i, 37.

[if you ask my opinion, it is quite untrue that authority is firmer or more stable when it relies on force than when it is associated with affection.]*

I condemn all violence in the education of tender minds which are being trained for honour and freedom. In rigour and constraint there is always something servile, and I hold that you will never achieve by force what you cannot achieve by reason, intelligence and skill.

That was the way I was brought up. They tell me that I tasted the rod only twice during all my childhood, and that was but lightly. I owed the same treatment to the children born to me; they all die, though, before they are weaned. But Leonor, an only daughter who has escaped that calamity, has reached the age of six or more (her mother's gentleness readily predisposing her that way) without our having used in her upbringing and in the punishment of her childish faults anything but words – gentle ones at that. And even if my hopes for her turn out to be frustrated, there are other causes in plenty to blame for that without finding fault with my method of upbringing, which I know to be just and natural.

I would have been even more punctilious with boys, who are less born to serve and whose mode-of-being is freer: I would have loved to make their hearts overflow with openness and frankness. I have never seen caning achieve anything except making souls more cowardly or more maliciously stubborn.

Do we want to be loved by our children? Do we want

* Terence, *Adelphi*, I, i, 40–3.

to remove any occasion for their wishing us dead? – though no occasion for so horrible a wish could ever be right or pardonable: *'nullum scelus rationem habet'* [no crime has rational justification] – then let us within reason enrich their lives with whatever we have at our disposal. To achieve that we ought not to get married so young that our adult years almost become confounded with theirs. Such unseemliness can plunge us into many great difficulties – I mean especially in the case of the nobility, whose way of life is one of leisure and who can live, as we say, on their income. In other cases, where life is a struggle for money, the fellowship of a great many children is a help to the whole family; they are so many new ways and means of helping to enrich it.

I was thirty-three when I married; and I approve of thirty-five – the opinion attributed to Aristotle. Plato does not want any man to marry before thirty; he is also right to laugh at spouses who lie together after fifty-five, judging their offspring unworthy to live and eat.*

It was Thales who gave the right ages; his mother pressed him to get married when he was young: 'Too soon,' he said. When he was older: 'Too late!' Accept no time as opportune for any inopportune activity!

The Ancient Gauls reckoned it to be extremely reprehensible for a man to lie with a woman before he was twenty, particularly advising those who wanted to train for war to remain chaste well into adulthood, because sexual intercourse makes minds soft and deflects them.

---

* Aristotle, *Politics*, VII, xvi (age of thirty-seven not thirty-five); Plato, *Republic*, V, 460A ff.; cf. Tiraquellus, *De legibus connubialibus*, VI, §§ 44–7; 52.

Ma hor congiunto a giovinetta sposa,
Lieto homai de' figli, era invilito
Ne gli affetti di padre e di marito.

[But now, married to a young wife, happy to have children, he was weakened by his love as father and husband.]*

The history of Greece notes how Iccus of Tarentum, Chryso, Astylus, Diopompus and others deprived themselves of any sort of sexual activity during all the time they were getting their bodies in trim for the races, wrestling and other contests at the Olympic Games.†

Muley Hassan, the Dey of Tunis (the one whom the Emperor Charles V restored to his throne) was critical of his father's memory because he was always with his wives, calling him a weak effeminate spawner of children.

In a certain province in the Spanish Indies men were allowed to marry only after forty, yet girls could marry at ten.‡

If a nobleman is only thirty-five it is too soon for him to make way for a twenty-year-old son: he has still got to achieve a reputation in military expeditions or at the Court of his monarch: he needs his cash; he should allow his son a share but not forget himself. Such a man can rightly give the answer which fathers often have on their

---

* Plutarch, *Life of Thales*; Caesar, *Gallic Wars*, VI (cf. Tiraquellus, ibid., VI, § 47); Torquato Tasso, *Gierusalemme liberata*, X, 39–41.
† Tiraquellus, ibid., XV, § 26, citing Plato, *Laws*, VIII, 839E–840A.
‡ Paolo Giovio, *Historia sui temporis*, on 'Muleasses' (Muley Hassan); Lopez de Gomara, *Histoire générale des Indes*.

lips: 'I have no wish to be stripped bare before I go and lie down'. But a father who is brought low by age and illness, whose weakness and ill-health deprive him of ordinary human fellowship, does wrong to himself and to his family if he broods over a great pile of riches. If he is wise, he has reached the period when he really ought to want to get stripped and lie down – not stripped to his shirt but down to a nice warm dressing-gown. He has no more use for all the remaining pomp: he should give it all away as a present to those whom it ought to belong to by Nature's ordinance.

It is right that he should let them use what Nature deprives him of: otherwise there is certainly an element of malice and envy. The finest gesture the Emperor Charles V ever made was when, in imitation of some ancient holders of his rank, he was able to recognize that reason clearly commands us to strip off our garments when they weigh us down and get in our way, and to go and lie down when our legs fail us. Once he began to feel deficient in the strength and energy needed to continue to conduct his affairs with the glory he had earned, he handed over his wealth, his rank and his power to his son:

> *Solve senescentem mature sanus equum, ne*
> *Peccet ad extremum ridendus, et ilia ducat.*

[Be wise enough to unharness that tired old nag lest it ends up short-winded, stumbling while men jeer at it.]*

---

* Horace, *Epistles*, I, i, 8. (The 'old nag' is his Muse: hence the following development.)

This defect of not realizing in time what one is, of not being aware of the extreme decline into weakness which old age naturally brings to our bodies and our souls – to them equally in my opinion unless the soul actually has the larger share – has ruined the reputation of most of the world's great men. I have seen in my lifetime and intimately known great men in authority who had clearly declined amazingly from their former capacities, which I knew of from the reputation they had acquired in their better years. For their honour's sake I would deeply have wished that they had withdrawn to their estates, dropping the load of public or military affairs which were no longer meant for their shoulders.

There was a nobleman whose house I used to frequent who was a widower, very old but still with some sap in him. He had several daughters to marry and a son already old enough to enter society, so that his house was burdened with considerable expenditure and quite a lot of outside visitors; he took little pleasure in this, not only out of concern for economy but even more because, at his age, he had adopted a mode of life far different from ours. In that rather bold way I have I told him one day that it would be more becoming if he made room for us youth, leaving his principal residence to his son (for it was the only one properly equipped and furnished) and withdrew to a neighbouring estate of his where nobody would trouble his rest, since, given his children's circumstances, there was no other way he could avoid our unsuitable company. He later took my advice and liked it.

That is not to say we should make a binding gift of our property and not be able to go back on it. I am old enough to have to play that role now, and would leave the young the use of my house and property but be free to withdraw my consent if they gave me cause. I would let them have use of them because they no longer gave me pleasure, but I would retain as much general authority over affairs as I wanted to, for I have always thought that it must be a great happiness for an old father to train his own children in the management of his affairs; he could then, during his lifetime, observe how they do it, offering advice and instruction based on his own experience in such things, and personally arranging for the ancient honour and order of his house to come into the hands of his successors, confirming in this way the hopes he could place in their future management of them.

To do this I would not avoid their company; I would like to be near so as to watch them and to enjoy their fun and festivities as much as my age permitted. Even if I did not live among them (as I could not do without embarrassing the company by the gloominess of my age and by my being subject to illnesses – and also without being forced to restrict my own rules and habits), I would at least like to live near them in some corner of my house – not the fanciest but the most comfortable. Not (as I saw a few years ago) a dean of St-Hilaire-de-Poitiers brought to such a pitch of solitude by the troublesome effects of his melancholy that, when I went into his room, he had not set foot outside it for twenty-two years; yet he could still move about freely and easily, apart from a rheumatic flux discharging into his stomach. He would let scarcely anyone in to see him even once a week; he always stayed shut up in that room all by himself except for a valet who brought him his food once a day and who merely went in and out. His only occupation was to walk about reading a book (for he had some acquaintance with literature), obstinately determined as he was to die in those conditions – as soon afterwards he did.

I would try to have gentle relations with my children and so encourage in them an active love and unfeigned affection for me, something easily achieved in children of a well-born nature; of course if they turn out to be wild beasts (which our century produces in abundance) then you must hate them and avoid them as such.

I am against the custom of forbidding children to say 'Father' and requiring them to use some other, more respectful title, as though Nature had not sufficiently provided for our authority. We address God Almighty as Father and scorn to have our own children call us by that name.

It is also unjust, and mad, to deprive our grown-up children of easy relations with their fathers by striving to maintain an austere and contemptuous frown, hoping by that to keep them in fear and obedience. That is a quite useless farce which makes fathers loathsome to children and, what is worse, makes them ridiculous. Since youth and vigour are in their children's hands they enjoy the current favour of the world; they treat with mockery the fierce tyrannical countenance of a man with no blood left in his veins or his heart – scarecrows in a field of flax! Even if I were able to make myself feared I would rather make myself loved.

There are so many drawbacks in old age, so much powerlessness; it so merits contempt that the best endowment it can acquire is the fond love of one's family: its arms are no longer fear and commands.

I know one man who had a most imperious youth. Now that old age is coming upon him, despite trying to accept it as well as he can, he slaps and bites and swears – the stormiest master in France; he frets himself with cares and watchfulness: but it is all a farce which the family conspire in; the others have access to the best part of his granary, his cellar and even his purse: meanwhile he keeps the keys in his pouch, dearer to him than sight itself. While he is happy to keep so spare and thrifty a table, in various secret places in his house all is dissipation, gambling, prodigality and tales about his fits of temper and his precautions. Everybody is on the lookout against him. If some wretched servant happens to become devoted to him, suspicion is immediately thrown on to him – a quality which old age is only too ready to ruminate upon. How many times has that man boasted to me of keeping his family on a tight rein, of the meticulous obedience and reverence he received because of it, and of the lucid watch he kept over his affairs:

> *Ille solus nescit omnia!*
> [He alone is unaware of the lot!]*

---

* Terence, *Adelphi*, IV, ii, 9.

No man of my acquaintance can claim more qualities, natural and acquired, proper for maintaining his mastery; yet he had failed completely, like a child. That is why I have picked him out as an example from several other cases that I know.

It would make a good scholastic debate: whether or not he is better off as he is. In his presence, all things defer to him; his authority runs its empty course: nobody ever resists him; they believe what he says, they fear and respect him . . . as much as he could wish! Should he dismiss a servant he packs his bag and is off at once – but only out of his presence. Old people's steps are so slow and their senses so confused that the valet can live a full year in the house doing his duty without their even noticing it. At the appropriate time a letter arrives from distant parts, a pitiful one, a submissive one, full of promises to do better in the future; the valet then finds himself back in favour.

Does my Lord strike a bargain and send a missive which the family do not like? They suppress it, sometimes inventing afterwards reasons to explain the lack of action or reply. Since no letters from outside are ever brought to him first, he only sees the ones which it seems convenient for him to know. If he happens to get hold of any, he always has to rely on somebody else to read them for him, so they invent things on the spot: they are always pretending that someone is begging his pardon in the very letter that contains abuse. In short he sees his affairs only through some counterfeit image designed to be as pleasing to him as they can make it so as not to awake his spleen or his anger.

Under various guises, but all to the same effect, I have seen plenty of households run long and steadily in this way.

Wives are always disposed to disagree with their husbands. With both hands they grasp at any pretence for contradicting them; any excuse serves as full justification. I know one who used to rob her husband wholesale – in order, she told her confessor, to 'fatten up her alms-giving'. (There's a religious spendthrift for you to trust!) Whatever their husbands agree to never provides them with enough dignity. To give it grace and authority they must have usurped it by ruse or by force, but always unjustly. When, as in the case I am thinking of, they are acting against some poor old man on behalf of the children, they seize on this pretext and are honoured for serving their own passions; and, as though they were all slaves together, readily plot against his sovereignty and government. If the children are male and grown-up, in the bloom of youth, then their mothers gang up with them and corrupt the steward, the bursar and everyone else by force or favour.

Old men without wives and children fall into this evil less easily but more cruelly and with less dignity. Cato the Elder already said in his time, 'So many valets: so many enemies.' Given the gulf separating the purity of his century from ours, just think whether he was not really warning us that wife, sons and valet are all 'so many enemies' in our case.

It is a good thing that decrepitude furnishes us with the sweet gifts of inadvertency, ignorance and a readiness to be cheated. If we were to resist, what would happen to us, especially nowadays when the judges who settle our quarrels are usually on the side of the children – and venal?

The cheating may escape my sight, but it does not escape my sight that I am very cheatable. Thrice and four times blessed is he who can entrust his pitiful old age into the hands of a friend. And shall we have ever said enough about the value of a friend and how totally different it is from bonds based on contracts! Even that counterpart to a friend which I see between beasts, how devoutly I honour it! Am I better or worse off for having savoured a friend? Better off, certainly. My regret for him consoles me and honours me. Is it not a most pious and pleasant task in life to be ever performing his obsequies? Can any pleasure possessed equal that pleasure lost? I would readily let myself be rapt insensible lingering over so caressing a notion.

Others may deceive me, but at least I do not deceive myself into thinking that I can protect myself against it; nor do I cudgel my brains for ways of making myself able to do so. Only in my own bosom can I find salvation from treachery like this – not in disquieting and tumultuous inquisitiveness but in diversion and constancy. Whenever I hear of the state that some other man is in, I waste no time over that but immediately turn my eyes on to myself to see how I am doing. Everything which touches him touches me too. What has happened to him is a warning and an alert coming from the same quarter. Every day, every hour, we say things about others which ought more properly to be addressed to ourselves if only we had learned to turn our thoughts inward as well as widely outward. Similarly many authors inflict wounds on the cause they defend by dashing out against the attackers, hurling shafts at their enemies which can properly be hurled back at them.

The late Monsieur de Monluc, the Marshal, when talking to me of the loss of his son (a truly brave gentleman of great promise who died on the island of Madeira), among other regrets emphasized the grief and heartbreak he felt at never having revealed himself to his son and at having lost the pleasure of knowing and savouring him, all because of his fancy to appear with the gravity of a stern father; he had never told him of the immense love he felt for him and how worthy he rated him for his virtue. 'And all that poor boy saw of me,' he said, 'was a frowning face full of scorn; he is gone, believing I was unable to love him or to judge him as he deserved. Whom was I keeping it for, that knowledge of the special love I harboured for him in my soul! Should not he have felt all the pleasure of it, and all the bonds of gratitude? I forced myself, I tortured myself, to keep up that silly mask, thereby losing the joy of his company – and his goodwill as well, which must have been cold towards me: he had never received from me anything but brusqueness or known anything but a tyrannous façade.'

I find that lament to be reasonable and rightly held: for as I know only too well from experience when we lose those we love there is no consolation sweeter than the knowledge of having remembered to tell them everything and to have enjoyed the most perfect and absolute communication with them.

As much as I can I open myself to my own folk, and

am most ready to tell them or anyone else what I intend towards them and what is the judgement I make on them. I hasten to reveal myself, to make myself known, for I do not want them to be misled about me in any way whatsoever.

According to Caesar, among the customs peculiar to our ancient Gauls there was the following: sons were not presented to their fathers and never dared to appear in public with them until they had begun to bear arms, as if to signify that the time had now come for the fathers to admit them to their intimate acquaintance.*

Yet another abuse of paternal discretion which I have seen in my time is when fathers are not content with having deprived their children of their natural share of the property during their long lifetime, but then go and leave authority over all of it after their death to their widows, free to dispose of it at their pleasure. One lord I have known (among the highest officers of the Realm) could rightfully have expected to come into property worth fifty thousand crowns a year: yet he died in need, overwhelmed with debts at the age of fifty, while his mother, despite advanced senility, still enjoyed rights over the entire property under the will of his father, who himself had lived to be eighty.

To me that seems in no way reasonable.

For all that, I cannot see it helps much when a man whose affairs are prospering goes and seeks a wife who burdens him with a large dowry: no debt contracted outside the family is more ruinous to a household. My

* Caesar, *Gallic Wars*, VI, xviii.

ancestors have all followed this precept, most fittingly; so have I.

Yet those who warn us against marrying rich wives out of fear that they might be less beholden to us and more difficult wrongly lose a real advantage for a frivolous conjecture. If a woman is unreasonable it costs her no more to jump over one reason than another. Such women are most pleased with themselves when they are most in the wrong: it is the injustice which allures them; whereas for good women it lies in their virtuous deeds: the richer they are the more gracious they are, just as beautiful women are more willingly and more triumphantly chaste.

It is reasonable to let mothers run affairs until the sons are legally old enough to assume the responsibility; but the father has brought them up wrongly if (considering the normal weakness of the female) he could not expect them to be wiser and more competent than his wife once they have reached that age. But it would be even more unnatural to make mothers depend on the discretion of their sons. They should be given a provision generous enough to maintain their state according to the condition of their family and their age, especially since want or indigence are far more difficult for them to bear with decorum than for males: that burden ought to be put on the sons rather than on the mother.

On the whole, the soundest way of sharing out our property when we die is (I believe) to follow local customary law. The Law has thought it out better than we have, so it is better to let the Law make the wrong choice than rashly hazard doing so ourselves. The property does not really belong to us personally, since without our leave it is entailed by civil law to designated heirs. And even though we have some discretion as well, I hold that it would take a great and very clear reason to justify our depriving anyone of what he was entitled to by the fortune of his birth and of what common law leads him to expect; it would be an unreasonable abuse of that freedom to make it serve whims both frivolous and private.

Fate has been kind, sparing me opportunities which might have tempted me to change my predilection for the dictates of common law. I know people whom it would be a waste of time to serve long and dutifully: one word taken the wrong way can wipe out ten years of merit. Anyone able to butter them up when they are just about to go is lucky indeed! The latest action scoops the lot: it is not the best and most frequent services which prove efficacious but recent ones, present ones.

There are people who exploit their wills as sticks and carrots to punish or reward every action of those who may claim an interest in the inheritance. But this is a matter of long-lasting consequence; it is too weighty to be changed from moment to moment: wise men settle it once and for all – and have regard for the reasonable customs of the community.

We are a little too fond of male entail; we foresee a ridiculous eternity for our family name and attach too much weight to silly conjectures about the future based on the minds of little boys. Somebody might easily have been unjust to me, ousting me from my place because I was more lumpish, more leaden, more slow and more unwilling to learn than any of my brothers (indeed, than all the children in my province), whether I was being taught to exercise mind or body. It is madness to make such selections, interrupting the succession on the faith of such fortune-telling which has so often deceived us. If we can ever infringe that rule and correct the choice of heirs made by destiny, it would probably be out of consideration for some huge noticeable physical deformity, of a permanent and incurable kind, one which those of us who are great admirers of beauty believe to be highly deleterious.

There is an agreeable dialogue between Plato's Lawgiver and his citizens which may honour my pages here: 'What!' they say, feeling their end draw near: 'Can we not bequeath our own property to anyone we please? What cruelty, O gods, that it be not lawful to give more or to give less just as we like, depending on how our heirs have helped us in our affairs, our illnesses or our old age!' The Legislator made this reply: 'My dear friends; you are certain to die soon: so it is difficult for any of you to "Know Thyself" (according to that Delphic inscription) and to know what is yours. I make these laws and maintain that you do not belong to yourselves, nor do the things of which you enjoy the use actually belong to you. You and your goods belong to your family, both past and future. And still more do your family and your goods belong to the commonwealth. Therefore if on your sickbed or in your old age some flatterer tries to persuade you to make an unjust will (or if a fit of temper does) I will protect you. Out of respect for the general concerns of our City and of your family,

I will establish laws which make it known that private interests must reasonably yield to those of the community. Go, gently and willingly, whither human necessity bids you. It is for me, who favour all things equally and who take care of the people in general, to take care also of what you leave behind you.'*

To return to my subject, it seems to me right, somehow, that women should have no mastery over men save only the natural one of motherhood – unless it be for the chastisement of those who have wilfully submitted to them out of some feverish humour; but that does not apply to old women, the subject of our present discussion. It is the manifest truth of this consideration which has made us so ready to invent and entrench that Salic Law – which nobody has ever seen – which debars women from succeeding to our throne; and though Fortune has lent it more credence in some places than others, there is scarcely one jurisdiction in the world where that law is not cited as here, because of the genuine appearance of reason which gives it authority.

It is dangerous to leave the superintendence of our succession to the judgement of our wives and to their choice between our sons, which over and over again is iniquitous and fantastic. For those unruly tastes and physical cravings which they experience during pregnancy are ever-present in their souls. They regularly devote themselves to the weakest and to the feeblest, or to those (if they have any) who are still hanging about their necks. Since women do not have sufficient reason-

* Plato, *Laws*, XI, 922 D–924 A.

ing-power to select and embrace things according to their merits they allow themselves to be led to where natural impressions act most alone – like animals, which only know their young while they are still on the teat.

Incidentally, experience clearly shows us that the natural love to which we attach such importance has very shallow roots. For a very small sum of money we daily tear their own children out of women's arms and get them to take charge of our own; we make them entrust their babes to some wretched wet-nurse to whom we have no wish to commit our own or else to a nanny-goat; then we forbid them not only to give suck to theirs no matter what harm it might do them but even to look after them; they must devote themselves entirely to the service of our children. And then we see that in most cases custom begets a kind of bastard love more distracted than the natural kind; they are far more worried about the preservation of those foster-children than of the children who really belong to them.

I mentioned nanny-goats because the village-women where I live call in the help of goats when they cannot suckle their children themselves; I have now two menservants who never tasted mothers' milk for more than a week. These nanny-goats are trained from the outset to suckle human children; they recognize their voices when they start crying and come running up. They reject any other child you give them except the one they are feeding; the child does the same to another nanny-goat. The other day I saw an infant who had lost its own nanny-goat as the father had only borrowed it from a neighbour: the child rejected a different one which was provided and died, certainly of hunger.

The beasts debase and bastardize maternal affection as easily as we do.

Herodotus tells of a certain district of Libya where men lie with women indiscriminately, but where, once a child can toddle, it recognizes its own father out of the crowd, natural instinct guiding its first footsteps.* There are frequent mistakes, I believe . . .

Now once we consider the fact that we love our children simply because we begot them, calling them our second selves, we can see that we also produce something else from ourselves, no less worthy of commendation: for the things we engender in our soul, the offspring of our mind, of our wisdom and talents, are the products of a part more noble than the body and are more purely our own. In this act of generation we are both mother and father; these 'children' cost us dearer and, if they are any good, bring us more honour. In the case of our other children their good qualities belong much more to them than to us: we have only a very slight share in them; but in the case of these, all their grace, worth and beauty belong to us. For this reason they have a more lively resemblance and correspondence to us. Plato adds that such children are immortal and immortalize their fathers – even deifying them, as in the case of Lycurgus, Solon and Minos.†

* Tiraquellus, *De legibus connubialibus*, VII, § 51; Herodotus, *History*, IV.

† Plato, *Phaedrus*, 258 C, dealing with a man's writings, his 'brain-children'; but Montaigne has transcribed *Minos* for *Darius*.

Since our history books are full of exemplary cases of the common kind of paternal love, it seemed to me not inappropriate to cite a few examples of this other kind too.

Heliodorus, that good bishop of Tricca, preferred to forgo the honour of so venerable a bishopric with its income and its dignity rather than to destroy his 'daughter', who still lives on – a handsome girl but attired perhaps with a little more care and indulgence than suits the daughter of a priest, of a clerk in holy orders – and fashioned in too erotic a style.

In Rome there was a figure of great bravery and dignity called Labienus; among other qualities he excelled in every kind of literature; he was, I think, the son of that great Labienus who was the foremost among captains who served under Caesar in the Gallic Wars, subsequently threw in his lot with Pompey the Great and fought for him most bravely until Caesar defeated him in Spain. There were several people who were jealous of the Labienus I am referring to; he also probably had enemies among the courtiers and favourites of the contemporary Emperors for his frankness and for inheriting his father's innate hostility towards tyranny, which we may believe coloured his books and writing. His enemies prosecuted him before the Roman magistrates and obtained a conviction, requiring several of the books he had published to be burnt. This was the very first case of the death-penalty being inflicted on books and erudition; it was subsequently applied at Rome in several other cases. We did not have means nor matter enough for our cruelty unless we also let it concern itself with things which Nature has exempted from any sense of pain, such as our renown and the products of our minds, and unless we inflicted physical suffering on the teachings and the documents of the Muses.

Labienus could not bear such a loss nor survive such beloved offspring; he had himself borne to the family vault on a litter and shut up alive; there he provided his own death and burial. It is difficult to find any example of fatherly love more vehement than that one. When his very eloquent friend Cassius Severus saw those books being burnt, he shouted that he too ought to be burnt alive with them since he actively preserved their contents in his memory.

A similar misfortune happened to Greuntius Cordus who was accused of having praised Brutus and Cassius in his books. That slavish base and corrupt Senate (worthy of a worse master than Tiberius) condemned his writings to the pyre: it pleased him to keep his books company as they perished in the flames by starving himself to death.

Lucan was a good man, condemned by that black-guard Nero; in the last moments of his life, when most of his blood had already gushed from his veins (he had ordered his doctors to kill him by slashing them) and when cold had already seized his hands and feet and was starting to draw near to his vital organs, the very last thing he remembered were some verses from his *Pharsalian War*; he recited them, and died with them as the last words on his lips. Was that not saying farewell to his children tenderly and paternally, the equivalent of those adieus and tender embraces which we keep for our children when we die, as well as being an effect of that natural instinct to recall at our end those things which we held dearest to us while we lived?

When Epicurus lay dying, tormented they say by the most extreme colic paroxysms, he found consolation only in the beauty of the philosophy he had taught to the world;* are we to believe that he would have found happiness in any number of well-born, well-educated children (if he had had any) to equal what he found in the abundant writing which he had brought forth? And if he had had the choice of leaving either an ill-conceived and deformed child behind him or a stupid and inept book, would – not he alone but any man of similar ability – have preferred to incur the first tragedy rather than the other?

It would probably have been impious of Saint Augustine (for example) if someone had obliged him to destroy either his children (supposing he had had any) or else his writings (from which our religion receives such abundant profit) and he had not preferred to destroy his children.

I am not at all sure whether I would not much rather have given birth to one perfectly formed son by commerce with the Muses than by commerce with my wife. As for this present child of my brain, what I give it I give unconditionally and irrevocably, just as one does to the children of one's body; such little good as I have already done it is no longer mine to dispose of; it may know plenty of things which I know no longer, and remember things about me that I have forgotten; if the need arose

* Cicero, *De finibus*, II, xxx, 96.

to turn to it for help, it would be like borrowing from a stranger. It is richer than I am, yet I am wiser than it.

Few devotees of poetry would not have been more gratified at fathering the *Aeneid* than the fairest boy in Rome, nor fail to find the loss of one more bearable than the other. For according to Aristotle, of all artists the one who is most in love with his handiwork is the poet.*

It is hard to believe that Epaminondas (who boasted that his posterity consisted in two 'daughters' who would bring honour to their father one day – he meant his two noble victories over the Spartans) would have agreed to exchange them for daughters who were the most gorgeous in the whole of Greece; or that Alexander and Caesar had ever wished they could give up the greatness of their glorious feats in war in return for the pleasure of having sons and heirs however perfect, however accomplished; indeed I very much doubt whether Phidias or any other outstanding sculptor would have found as much delight in the survival and longevity of his physical children as in some excellent piece of sculpture brought to completion by his long-sustained labour and his skill according to the rules of his art.

And as for those raging vicious passions which have sometimes inflamed fathers with love for their daughters, or mothers for their sons, similar ones can be found in this other kind of parenthood: witness the tale of Pygmalion who, having carved the statue of a uniquely beautiful woman, was so hopelessly ravished by an

* Aristotle, *Nicomachaean Ethics*, IX, vii, 3.

insane love for his own work that, for the sake of his frenzy, the gods had to bring her to life:

> *Tentatum mollescit ebur, positoque rigore*
> *Subsedit digitis.*

[He touches the ivory statue; it starts to soften; its hardness gone, it yields to his fingers.]*

* Ovid, *Metamorphoses*, X, 243 ff., citing 283–4.

6

On moderation

It is as though our very touch bore infection: things
which in themselves are good and beautiful are corrupted
by our handling of them. We can seize hold even of
Virtue in such a way that our action makes her vicious
if we clasp her in too harsh and too violent an embrace.
Those who say that Virtue knows no excess (since she is
no longer Virtue if there is excess within her) are merely
playing with words.

> *Insani sapiens nomen ferat, aequus iniqui,*
> *Ultra quam satis est virtutem si petat ipsam*

[The name of 'insane' is borne by the Sage and the name of
'unjust' is borne by the Just, if in their strivings after Virtue
herself they go beyond what is sufficient.]*

That is a subtle observation on the part of philosophy:
you can both love virtue too much and behave with
excess in an action which itself is just. The Voice of God
adapts itself fittingly to that bias: 'Be not more wise than
it behoveth, but be ye soberly wise.'†

---

* Horace, *Epistles*, I, vi, 15–16.
† Romans 12:3, following the Vulgate Latin version in which Montaigne read his Bible.

I have seen one of our great noblemen harm the reputation of his religion by showing himself religious beyond any example of men of his rank.*

I like natures which are temperate and moderate. Even when an immoderate zeal for the good does not offend me it still stuns me and makes it difficult for me to give it a Christian name. Neither Pausanias' mother (who made the first accusation against her son and who brought the first stone to wall him up for his death) nor Posthumius (the Dictator who had his own son put to death because he had been carried away by youthful ardour and had fought – successfully – slightly ahead of his unit) seem 'just' to me: they seem odd.† I neither like to advise nor to imitate a virtue so savage and so costly: the archer who shoots beyond his target misses it just as much as the one who falls short; my eyes trouble me as much when I suddenly come up into a strong light as when I plunge into darkness.

Callicles says in Plato‡ that, at its extremes, philosophy is harmful; he advises us not to go more deeply into it than the limits of what is profitable: taken in moderation philosophy is pleasant and useful, but it can eventually lead to a man's becoming vicious and savage, contemptuous of religion and of the accepted laws, an enemy of social intercourse, an enemy of our human pleasures, useless at governing cities, at helping others or even at helping himself – a man whose ears you could box with impunity. What he says is true, for in its excesses

---

* Perhaps King Henry III.   † Diodorus Siculus, XI, x; XII, xix.
‡ Plato, *Gorgias*, 484C–D.

philosophy enslaves our native freedom and with untimely subtleties makes us stray from that beautiful and
easy path that Nature has traced for us.

The affection which we bear towards our wives is
entirely legitimate: yet Theology nevertheless puts reins
on it and restrains it. Among the reasons which Saint
Thomas Aquinas* cites in condemnation of marriages
between relatives who are within the forbidden affinities
I think I once read the following: There is a risk that the
love felt for such a wife might be immoderate; for if the
marital affection between them is full and entire (as it
ought to be) and then you add on to it the further
affection proper among kinsfolk, there is no doubt that
such an over-measure would ravish such a husband
beyond the limits of reason.

Those sciences which govern the morals of mankind,
such as Theology and philosophy, make everything their
concern: no activity is so private or so secret as to escape
their attention or their jurisdiction. Only mere beginners
criticize their freedom to do so: they are like the kind of
women whose organs are as accessible as you wish for
copulation but who are too bashful to show them to the
doctor. On behalf of these sciences I therefore want to
teach husbands the following – if, that is, there are any
who are still too eager: even those very pleasures which
they enjoy when lying with their wives are reproved if
not kept within moderation; you can fall into licence and
excess in this as in matters unlawful. All those shameless
caresses which our first ardour suggests to us in our

* Thomas Aquinas, *Summa theologica*, II^a, II^{ac}, 154, art. 9.

sex-play are not only unbecoming to our wives but harmful to them when practised on them. At least let them learn shamelessness from some other hand! They are always wide enough awake when we need them. Where this is concerned what I have taught has been natural and uncomplicated.

Marriage is a bond both religious and devout: that is why the pleasure we derive from it must be serious, restrained and intermingled with some gravity; its sensuousness should be somewhat wise and dutiful. Its chief end is procreation, so there are those who doubt whether it is right to seek intercourse when we have no hope of conception, as when the woman is pregnant or too old. For Plato that constitutes a kind of homicide. There are whole peoples, including the Mahometans, who abominate intercourse with women who are pregnant, and others still during monthly periods. Zenobia admitted her husband for a single discharge; once that was over she let him run wild throughout her pregnancy, giving him permission to begin again only once it was over. There was a fine and noble-hearted marriage for you!*

It was from some yearning sex-starved poet that Plato borrowed his story about Jupiter's making such heated advances to his wife one day that he could not wait for her to lie on the bed but tumbled her on the floor, forgetting the great and important decisions which he had just reached with the other gods in his celestial

* Plato, *Laws*, VIII, 838A ff.; Guillaume Postel, *Histoire des Turcs*; for Zenobia, Tiraquellus, *De legibus connubialibus*, IX, 88.

Court and boasting that he had enjoyed it as much as when, hidden from her parents, he had first taken her maidenhead.*

The kings of Persia did invite their wives as guests to their festivities, but once the wine had seriously inflamed them so that they had to let their lust gallop free, they packed them off to their quarters so as not to make them accomplices of their immoderate appetites, sending instead for other women whom they were not bound to respect.†

It is not every pleasure or favour that is well lodged in people of every sort. Epaminondas had a dissolute boy put in prison: Pelopidas, for his own purposes, begged for his freedom; Epaminondas refused but granted it to one of his whores who also begged for it, saying that it was a favour due to a mistress but not to a captain. Sophocles, when a Praetor with Pericles, happened to see a handsome youth go by: 'What a handsome boy,' said he to Pericles. 'That', said Pericles, 'would be all right coming from anyone but a Praetor, who must not only have pure hands but pure eyes.'‡

When the wife of the Emperor Aelius Verus complained of his permitting himself affairs with other women, he replied that he acted thus for reasons of conscience, marriage being a term of honour and dignity not of wanton and lascivious lust. And our old Church

---

* Plato, *Laws*, III, 390 BC, after Homer, *Iliad*, XIV, 294–341.

† Plutarch (tr. Amyot), *Préceptes de mariage*, 146E.

‡ Plutarch (tr. Amyot), *Instruction pour ceux qui manient les affaires d'Estat*, 167 H; Cicero, *De officiis*, I, xl, 144, distinguishing between moderation (*modestia*) and orderly conduct (*eutaxia*).

authors make honourable mention of a wife who rejected her husband since she had no wish to be a partner to his lascivious and immoderate embraces.*

In short there is no pleasure, however proper, which does not become a matter of reproach when excessive and intemperate.

But, seriously though, is not Man a wretched creature? Because of his natural attributes he is hardly able to taste one single pleasure pure and entire: yet he has to go and curtail even that by arguments; he is not wretched enough until he has increased his wretchedness by art and assiduity.

> *Fortunae miseras auximus arte vias.*
> [The wretched paths of Fortune we make worse by art.]†

Human wisdom is stupidly clever when used to diminish the number and sweetness of such pleasures as do belong to us, just as she employs her arts with diligence and fitness when she brings comb and cosmetics to our ills and makes us feel them less. If I had founded a school of philosophy I would have taken another route – a more natural one, that is to say a true, convenient and inviolate one; and I might have made myself strong enough to know when to stop.

Consider the fact that those physicians of our souls and bodies, as though plotting together, can find no other way to cure us and no other remedy for our

---

* E.g., Eusebius (*Pamphilus*), *Ecclesiastical History*, IV.
† Propertius, III, vii, 32.

illnesses of soul and body than by torment, pain and tribulation. Vigils, fasting, hair-shirts and banishments to distant solitary places, endless imprisonments, scourges and other sufferings have been brought in to that end: but only on condition that the suffering is real and should cause bitter pain, and that there should not befall what happened to a man called Gallio who was banished to the island of Lesbos: Rome was told that he was enjoying himself there and that what had been inflicted as a punishment was turning into a pleasure, at which he was ordered back to wife and home and commanded to stay put, so as to adapt the punishment to his real feelings.* For if a man's health and happiness were made keener by fasting, or if he found fish more tasty than meat, it would cease to be a salutary prescription: just as drugs prescribed by the other kind of doctor have no effect on anyone who swallowed them with pleasure and enjoyment. The bitter taste and the hardship are attributes which make them work. A constitution which could regularly stand rhubarb would spoil its efficacy: to cure our stomachs it must be something which hurts it: and here the usual axiom that 'contraries cure contraries' breaks down; for in this case illness cures illness.

This notion is somewhat like that other very ancient one which was universally embraced by all religions and which leads us to think that we can please Heaven and Nature by our murders and our massacres.

Even in our fathers' time Amurath, when he conquered the Isthmus, sacrificed six hundred Greek youths

---

* The Senator Junius Gallio; cf. Tacitus, *Annals*, VI, iii.

for the soul of his father, so that their blood might serve as a propitiation, expiating the sins of that dead man.* And in those new lands discovered in our own time, lands pure and virgin compared with ours, the practice is accepted virtually everywhere: all their idols are slaked with human blood, not without various examples of dreadful cruelty. Men are burned alive; when half-roasted they are withdrawn from the fire so that their hearts and entrails can be plucked out; others, even women, are flayed alive: their skin, all bloody, serves as a cloak to mask others; and there are no less examples of constancy and determination. For those wretches who are to be immolated, old men, women and children, beg for alms a few days beforehand as offertories at their sacrifice, and present themselves to the slaughter singing and dancing with the congregation. The ambassadors from the King of Mexico, to make Fernando Cortez realize the greatness of their master, first told him that he had thirty vassal-lords, each one of whom could muster a hundred thousand fighting men, and that he dwelt in the strongest fairest city under Heaven; they then added that he had fifty thousand men sacrificed to the gods every year. It is truly said that he cultivated war with some great neighbouring peoples not merely to train the youth of his country but chiefly to furnish prisoners of war for his sacrifices. In another place there was a town where they welcomed Cortez by sacrificing fifty men at the same time. And I will relate one more

* Related by Laonicus Chalcocondylas (tr. Blaise de Vigenère), *Histoire de la décadence de l'empire grec*, VII, iv.

account: when Cortez had conquered some of these peoples they sent messengers to find out about him and to seek his friendship. They offered him three sorts of gifts in this wise: 'Lord, here are five slaves; if thou art a fierce god who feedest on flesh and blood, eat them and we shall bring thee more. If thou art a kindly god, here are feathers and incense; if thou art human, accept these birds and these fruits.'*

---

* All from Francisco Lopez de Gomara, *Historia de Mexico*, Antwerp, 1554 (tr. A. de Cravaliz as *Historia del Capitano Don Fernando Cortes*, Rome, 1556).

7

That we should not be deemed happy till after our death

Scilicet ultima semper
Expectanda dies homini est, dicique beatus
Ante obitum nemo, supremaque funera debet.
[You must always await a man's last day: before his death and
last funeral rites, no one should be called happy.]*

There is a story about this which children know; it
concerns King Croesus: having been taken by Cyrus
and condemned to death, he cried out as he awaited
execution, 'O Solon, Solon!' This was reported to Cyrus
who inquired of him what it meant. Croesus explained
to him that Solon had once given him a warning which
he was now proving true to his own cost: that men, no
matter how Fortune may smile on them, can never be
called happy until you have seen them pass through the
last day of their life, on account of the uncertainty and
mutability of human affairs which lightly shift from state
to state, each one different from the other. That is why
Agesilaus replied to someone who called the King of
Persia happy because he had come so young to so great

* Ovid, *Metamorphoses*, III, 135.

an estate, 'Yes: but Priam was not wretched when he was that age.'* Descendants of Alexander the Great, themselves kings of Macedonia, became cabinet-makers and scriveners in Rome; tyrants of Sicily became school-teachers in Corinth. A conqueror of half the world, a general of numerous armies, became a wretched suppli-ant to the beggarly officials of the King of Egypt: that was the cost of five or six more months of life to Pompey the Great. And during our fathers' lifetime Ludovico Sforza, the tenth Duke of Milan, who for so long had been the driving force in Italy, was seen to die prisoner at Loches – but (and that was the worst of it) only after living there ten years. The fairest Queen, widow of the greatest King in Christendom, has she not just died by the hand of the executioner?† There are hundreds of other such examples. For just as storms and tempests seem to rage against the haughty arrogant height of our buildings, so it could seem that there are spirits above us, envious of any greatness here below.

> *Usque adeo res humanas vis abdita quaedam*
> *Obterit, et pulchros fasces saevasque secures*
> *Proculcare, ac ludibrio sibi habere videtur.*

[Some hidden force apparently topples the affairs of men, seeming to trample down the resplendent fasces and the lictor's unyielding axe, holding them in derision.]‡

---

* Plutarch, tr. Amyot, *Dicts notables des Lacedaemoniens*, p. 211C.

† Ludovico Sforza, ousted in 1500, spent *eight* years in the dungeon at Loches; Mary Stuart (widow of Francis II of France) was beheaded in 1587.

‡ Lucretius, V, 1233. (The *fasces* and *axes* were Roman symbols of State.)

Fortune sometimes seems precisely to lie in ambush for the last day of a man's life in order to display her power to topple in a moment what she had built up over the length of years, and to make us follow Laberius and exclaim: '*Nimirum hac die una plus vixi, mihi quam vivendum fuit.*' [I have lived this day one day longer than I ought to have lived.]*

The good counsel of Solon could be taken that way. But he was a philosopher: for such, the favours and ill graces of Fortune do not rank as happiness or unhappiness and for them great honours and powers are non-essential properties, counted virtually as things indifferent. So it seems likely to me that he was looking beyond that, intending to tell us that happiness in life (depending as it does on the tranquillity and contentment of a spirit well-born and on the resolution and assurance of an ordered soul) may never be attributed to any man until we have seen him act out the last scene in his play, which is indubitably the hardest. In all the rest he can wear an actor's mask: those fine philosophical arguments may be only a pose, or whatever else befalls us may not assay us to the quick, allowing us to keep our countenance serene. But in that last scene played between death and ourself there is no more feigning; we must speak straightforward French; we must show whatever is good and clean in the bottom of the pot:

> *Nam verae voces tum demum pectore ab imo*
> *Ejiciuntur, et eripitur persona, manet res*

* Macrobius, *Saturnalia*, II, vii.

[Only then are true words uttered from deep in our breast. The mask is ripped off: reality remains.]*

That is why all the other actions in our life must be tried on the touchstone of this final deed. It is the Master-day, the day which judges all the others; it is (says one of the Ancients)† the day which must judge all my years now past. The assay of the fruits of my studies is postponed unto death. Then we shall see if my arguments come from my lips or my heart.

I note that several men by their death have given a good or bad reputation to their entire life. Scipio, Pompey's father-in-law, redeemed by a good death the poor opinion people had had of him until then. And when asked which of three men he judged most worthy of honour, Chabrias, Iphicrates or himself, Epaminondas replied, 'Before deciding that you must see us die.' (Indeed Epaminondas would be robbed of a great deal if anyone were to weigh his worth without the honour and greatness of his end.)

In my own times three of the most execrable and ill-famed men I have known, men plunged into every kind of abomination, died deaths which were well-ordered and in all respects perfectly reconciled: such was God's good pleasure.

Some deaths are fine and fortunate. I knew a man‡ whose thread of life was progressing towards brilliant preferment when it was snapped; his end was so splendid

---

* Lucretius, III, 57.   † Seneca, *Epist. moral.*, XXIV and XXVI.
‡ Etienne de La Boëtie.

that, in my opinion, his great-souled search after honour held nothing so sublime as that snapping asunder: the goal he aimed for he reached before he had even set out; that was more grand and more glorious than anything he had wished or hoped for. As he fell he surpassed the power and reputation towards which his course aspired.

When judging another's life I always look to see how its end was borne: and one of my main concerns for my own is that it be borne well – that is, in a quiet and muted manner.